"The sweetness of the gos[...] not deserve him. He loves [...] wants. He is not embarrassed by embarrassing people. This is good news, especially for messed-up people like you and me. *He Is Not Ashamed* welcomes you to come face-to-face with the Jesus who doesn't shame sinners but summons them to be part of his forever family. Whether you're just coming to know Jesus or have walked with him for decades, I commend this wonderful work to you."

J. Garrett Kell, Lead Pastor, Del Ray Baptist Church, Alexandria, Virginia; author, *Pure in Heart*

"Our past, present, and potential future can often cause us to believe we aren't worthy of God's love. And the truth is, we aren't. This is what makes God's love through Christ genuinely amazing—it's freely extended to the unworthy, outcast, and overlooked. *He Is Not Ashamed* is a thoroughly biblical and experiential portrait of the love, tenderness, and grace Christ extends to all his beloved people, regardless of how we sometimes feel about ourselves. Erik Raymond turns our gaze from our constant introspection to the magnificent wonder of divine love. Wherever you are or whatever you've done, these words will undoubtedly be fresh water for your parched soul."

Dustin Benge, Associate Professor of Biblical Spirituality and Historical Theology, The Southern Baptist Theological Seminary; author, *The Loveliest Place*

"Erik Raymond has given us a masterful treatment of the most staggering reality in human existence. *He Is Not Ashamed* is like a tall, full glass of cool water for anyone that is dry and thirsty for grace."

Jared C. Wilson, Assistant Professor of Pastoral Ministry, Midwestern Baptist Theological Seminary; author, *Love Me Anyway*

"*He Is Not Ashamed* might just convince you that the good news about Jesus is even better than you dared to believe. Erik Raymond demonstrates from the Scriptures that Jesus loves his people more than they could imagine, despite our sin, weakness, and shame. It moved my heart with gratitude and joy, and it brought more than a few tears to my eyes. I cannot wait to pass it on to friends."

Michael McKinley, Senior Pastor, Sterling Park Baptist Church, Sterling, Virginia

"Do you believe that God loves you as he loves Christ? As a pastor of a local congregation, I have found that many Christians, including me, struggle to believe that God truly loves them in the way he says he does (John 17:23). It's only when we come to grasp God's staggering love for us that we will experience the deep humility, genuine freedom, and abundant life that we have in Christ. Understanding this naturally leads to a life of loving and grateful obedience to our Savior as we rest in his perfect righteousness, all by the power of the Holy Spirit. I am so grateful for pastor Erik Raymond and for this insightful book that helps us to ground ourselves in God's unchanging love for us rather than in the constantly changing emotions of our hearts."

Burk Parsons, Senior Pastor, Saint Andrew's Chapel, Sanford, Florida; Editor, *Tabletalk*

He Is Not Ashamed

He Is Not Ashamed

The Staggering Love of Christ for His People

Erik Raymond

WHEATON, ILLINOIS

Library of Congress Cataloging-in-Publication Data

Names: Raymond, Erik, author.
Title: He is not ashamed : the staggering love of Christ for his people / Erik Raymond.
Description: Wheaton, Illinois : Crossway, [2022] | Includes bibliographical references and index.
Identifiers: LCCN 2021035683 (print) | LCCN 2021035684 (ebook) | ISBN 9781433579349 (trade paperback) | ISBN 9781433579356 (pdf) | ISBN 9781433579363 (mobipocket) | ISBN 9781433579370 (epub)
Subjects: LCSH: God (Christianity)—Love. | Forgiveness of sin.
Classification: LCC BT140 .R39 2022 (print) | LCC BT140 (ebook) | DDC 231/.6—dc23
LC record available at https://lccn.loc.gov/2021035683
LC ebook record available at https://lccn.loc.gov/2021035684

To those who fill out the family photo of Jesus.
May you stand upright, with a smile formed by grace,
assured that Jesus not only knows you but loves you.

"If I ever reach heaven, I expect to find three wonders there:
first, to meet some I had not thought to see there;
second, to miss some I had expected to see there;
and third, the greatest wonder of all, to find myself there."

JOHN NEWTON

Contents

Acknowledgments

I AM GRATEFUL TO GOD for providing so many encouraging friends to help with this project. It has been a joy to partner with Crossway, an organization that reflects its biblical convictions not only with the content they produce but also with their diligence in ensuring it's done well. In particular, I'm indebted to Dave De-Witt and Todd Augustine for encouraging the book. Chris Cowan has been a rich blessing as an editor. I'm thankful for the support of my church family, Redeemer Fellowship Church, where I'm privileged to serve as a pastor. I'm indebted to many conversation partners who've provided thoughtful and clarifying feedback. I'm especially thankful for my friends, Andrew Belli, Dave Comeau, and Philip Van Steenburgh. They helped me wrestle through ideas, read the manuscript, and provided thoughtful feedback. I'm also thankful for my family's strong support and sacrifice for this project, especially my loving wife, Christie. Her encouragement to carve out a weekly writing rhythm was both wise and fruitful. This along with continued feedback and discussion are treasured. You are indeed an excellent wife more precious than any earthly treasure (Prov. 31:10).

Introduction

IMAGINE IF WE gathered together all of the believers throughout history and lined them up for a massive family photo. Whom would we see? What kinds of people would be there?

We may be surprised.

Dotting the horizon of this picture, we'd find people with unflattering stories. Some are known as the chief of sinners, the sinful woman, the thief on the cross, and the prostitute. We'd also see those who were overlooked and disregarded by society. We'd find weak people unable to give God anything. We'd even see those who wore the uniform of opposition to God. Here in the portrait of grace, we'd find a multitude of misfits. It would be quite the picture.

If this were your family, would you hang it on the wall or hide it in the attic?

Now zoom in closer. Focus on the middle of the picture. Jesus is there. Seems out of place, doesn't he? There, in this panorama of redemption, is Jesus, the perfect Son of God, wedged shoulder to shoulder with people marked by their depravity. Jesus, identifying with men, women, and children of all ages and backgrounds.

Bearing the scars that narrate their painful stories and sinful histories, they surround Jesus.

At first glance, we might think that Jesus doesn't belong with people like this. What business does majesty have with outcasts?

But poring over the Scriptures, we see something else. In this family photo, Jesus may seem out of place, but in reality he's exactly where he belongs. Even more, *he's right where he wants to be*. Instead of being ashamed of them, he calls them family.

Jesus wouldn't hide his family picture. He'd hang it on the wall.

What a staggering reality! How do we forget it? From beginning to end, the Bible includes emphatic examples of the types of people Jesus identifies with. Take, for instance, Jesus's family tree listed in genealogies in the New Testament. Matthew's list (Matt. 1:1–16) includes Judah, Tamar, Rahab, Bathsheba, and Manasseh. These aren't exactly the all-star cast members of the Old Testament. Why does he include them? Every name carries a generous portion of depravity, separation, and shame that mark all who would follow Jesus. These are the people that Jesus comes to identify with and save. Don't forget this vital truth: Jesus not only comes *from* sinful people, but he also comes *for* them. He's not ashamed of people like you and me (Heb. 2:11).

We need help remembering this. We rob ourselves of joy and Christ of glory when we forget where we came from and Christ's heart for us.

We Can Easily Forget Where We Came From

With each passing day, Christians move further away from the hour of their conversion. And it can become easy to forget where we came from. This is natural. Days tick by, as do months, years, and decades. Our minds are full of current burdens and recent memories. It's tough to recall the experiences and emotions that characterized our lives before.

So easy to forget, but so important that we remember.

The Bible constantly reminds us to look over our shoulder. Paul tells his readers to look back:

> And you were dead in the trespasses and sins in which *you once walked*, following the course of this world, following the prince of the power of the air, the spirit that is now at work in the sons of disobedience—among whom *we all once lived* in the passions of our flesh, carrying out the desires of the body and the mind, and *were by nature* children of wrath, like the rest of mankind. (Eph. 2:1–3)

He continues with this retrospective approach in Ephesians 2:11–12:

> Therefore *remember* that *at one time* you Gentiles in the flesh, called "the uncircumcision" by what is called the circumcision, which is made in the flesh by hands—*remember that you were* at that time separated from Christ, alienated from the commonwealth of Israel and strangers to the covenants of promise, having no hope and without God in the world.

Paul reminds these Christians of their hopelessness and helplessness apart from Christ. He opens up their spiritual biography and begins reading from the ugly pages of their past. His words remind all believers that our natural disposition was one of opposition to and alienation from God. We were fully engaged in a rebellious insurgency against him. Listening to the direction of the commander of this world, we fell in line and marched to his cadence. Our mission was to satisfy our flesh. In a word, this is depravity. Depravity describes who we were, which in turn explains what we did. We were depraved, so we lived in sin.

Several years ago, someone made a video clip of John Piper saying in a sermon, "I don't just do bad things, I am bad. And so are you," accompanied by music from Michael Jackson's "I'm Bad."[1] While the arrangement might make us laugh, the theological truth is dead on. Our natural status is alienation from and enmity with God (Rom. 5:10; Col. 1:21). Although some may sin in larger font (bigger, bolder, and more noticeable sins), we all have a past characterized by rebellion against God. We all have something written on the page. To say it another way, *none of us were as bad as we could've been, but we weren't as good as we should've been.* As he surveys the whole of human history (except Jesus), God declares, "None is righteous, no, not one" (Rom. 3:10), "for all have sinned and fall short of the glory of God" (Rom. 3:23).

Forget this truth, and we dull our spiritual senses. Our gratitude to God should correspond to our understanding of what we have been forgiven. If we are forgiven little, our love will be little. But if we have been forgiven much, then we will love much (Luke 7:47). And, the truth is, we all have been forgiven much. Consider the alienation we all once experienced. Because of our sin and God's holiness, we were infinitely separated from him.

1   "John Piper is Bad," YouTube video, October 5, 2006, https://www.youtube.com.

But God in Christ reconciled us to himself! How could we ever get over this?

When we look into the family photo of Jesus and consider the lives we see there, I am sure we'll notice people just like us. And this should encourage us. Jesus identifies with people like you and me.

We Can Easily Forget the Heart of Christ

In addition to forgetting our sin, we can forget Christ's heart. We can forget how he views his people. You can forget how he sees you. The types of people that attract Jesus make other people uncomfortable. Jesus is different. His heart is drawn to the battered and broken. Nobody has a story that can make Jesus blush. Our sin doesn't repel such a compassionate Savior. It attracts him. This is something religious people tend to forget. To them, Jesus is a scandal, not a Savior. We see this all over Luke's Gospel.

> And the Pharisees and their scribes grumbled at his disciples, saying, "Why do you eat and drink with tax collectors and sinners?" (Luke 5:30)

> The Son of Man has come eating and drinking, and you say, "Look at him! A glutton and a drunkard, a friend of tax collectors and sinners!" (7:34)

> Now when the Pharisee who had invited him saw this, he said to himself, "If this man were a prophet, he would have known who and what sort of woman this is who is touching him, for she is a sinner." (7:39)

And the Pharisees and the scribes grumbled, saying, "This man receives sinners and eats with them." (15:2)

And when they saw it, they all grumbled, "He has gone in to be the guest of a man who is a sinner." (19:7)

Let's make sure we're not following the playbook of the Pharisees and religious leaders who were scandalized by Jesus. Pharisees teach us to scoff at sinners. Jesus welcomes them. Jesus is the Savior we need: someone we can be honest with and trust that he will welcome us, someone with whom it's okay not to be okay, someone who's not ashamed of us. We need Jesus.

Read this slowly. Jesus "is not ashamed to call [us] brothers" (Heb. 2:11). Although Jesus has every reason to be ashamed of us, the staggering fact is that he isn't at all. We sometimes use family terms like *brother* or *sister* to communicate close relationships. It was no different at the time when Hebrews was written.[2] Whether you're male or female, *brother* means the same thing here. When Jesus calls us his brothers, he's communicating the removal of all barriers imposed by his superiority.

To put it another way, he's pulling us close to himself and publicly owning us as his own. What could be more encouraging than this? "No unworthiness in them, no misery upon them, shall ever hinder the Lord Christ from owning them and openly avowing

---

2   "In the Graeco-Roman world of the first century 'brother' was occasionally used for persons of comparable social status, but when a person from another level of society was called 'brother', social distinctions gave way to a sense of unity." Peter T. O'Brien, *The Letter to the Hebrews*, Pillar New Testament Commentary (Grand Rapids, MI: Eerdmans, 2010), 109.

them to be his brethren."[3] No matter what we've done or what we're going through, he'll never love us any less. This should give believers unspeakable joy!

What's behind this unflinching love?

His Eternal Oath

God's love for his people is unconditional. In other words, no one could merit such love for themselves. It's a gift of grace. Such love is humbling because it is undeserved and unearned. It's entirely beyond our grasp—even on our best days. But this love fortifies us too. God lavishes his love on people even though they don't deserve it. For our sin, we deserve judgment (Rom. 3:23; 6:23). Yet, in a shocking reversal, we are given salvation as a gift. The God who knows all things knew that our best day would still merit his wrath. He also knew that our worst day wasn't beyond his mercy. In eternity past, before he even created the world, God set his love on his people.

God communicates this eternal act to us with a covenant.[4] A covenant is an oath, or promise, with an obligation. This particular covenant is between the Father and the Son, promising and obligating themselves to lovingly redeem sinners. There is a sacred bond between members of the Trinity. The Father sent the Son to assume human nature (Heb. 2:10–14; 10:5–7), put himself under the law, and pay the penalty for sin for all of his people (Gal. 1:4; 4:4–5). The Father promised the Son that he'd support him in his work

---

3   John Owen, *An Exposition of the Epistle to the Hebrews,* vol. 20 of *The Works of John Owen*, ed. W. H. Goold (Edinburgh: Johnstone and Hunter, 1854), 423.

4   This paragraph has been adapted from Erik Raymond, "Burn Long Not Just Hot," *The Gospel Coalition*, February 17, 2021, https://www.thegospelcoalition.org/.

through the Holy Spirit, deliver him from death, seat him at the right hand of glory, and send the Holy Spirit to build the church (Ps. 16:8–11; Isa. 42:6–7; John 14:26; 15:26; Phil. 2:9–11). The Father promised the Son the reward of a people from every tribe, language, and nation and that he'd draw and keep them unto glory (Ps. 2:7; John 6:37–45; Rev. 5:9). This eternal pact between the members of the Trinity was compelled, accomplished, and secured by love.[5]

As Christians we often allow our circumstances to interpret God's character. If we are enduring a difficult season, we might be tempted to think that God is angry with us or distant. Shouldn't we instead see our circumstances in light of God's character? Our fluctuations don't change him. They can't. Our cool hearts can't chill his eternal love. As you perceive a growing sense of your sin, zoom out. Notice the rays of his love that cannot be eclipsed. The matter is settled in eternity between the unchanging, all-powerful members of the Trinity. Moved by love, the Father elected a people (Eph. 1:4) and gave them to his Son (John 17:6). When Jesus went to the cross, he knew whom he was purchasing. And he didn't keep the receipt.

His Solidarity with Us

Hebrews also shows us that Christ's solidarity with his people is a chief reason for why he's not ashamed of them, "For he who

---

5 We see a window into this covenantal outworking shortly before Christ's death. As Jesus prayed to his Father, he said, "I have manifested your name to the people whom you gave me out of the world. Yours they were, and you gave them to me" (John 17:6). Notice that they were first the Father's and then they were given to the Son. This gift was not given on this particular night but in eternity, along with the work he was given to do: "I glorified you on earth, having accomplished the work that you gave me to do" (17:4). Here we see the covenant working itself out in real-time, with the Son praying to the Father and reviewing the gift from his Father.

sanctifies and those who are sanctified all have one source. That is why he is not ashamed to call them brothers" (Heb. 2:11). The one who sanctifies is Jesus, and those who are sanctified are the people of God. The shared source is God. This is anchored in the truth of the covenant of redemption: Jesus is the Son of God who entered into an eternal oath to save sinners. In a time *before* time, Christ identified with us. God loved us.

Jesus is not ashamed of his people because they are the ones on whom God has set his love before the foundation of the world (Eph. 1:4–5). God's people are Christ's people (John 17:6). We are the children that God has given him (Heb. 2:13). Jesus is not ashamed of his family photo because he loves every single one of us. He is well aware of our baggage. And he loves us anyway. He treats us like family. He always has and always will. Nothing we think or do could ever overturn such divine love to his children.

Let's consider another aspect of this solidarity: Jesus's humanity. Let's not forget who Jesus is. When he became a man, he didn't stop being God. Although his flesh veiled his infinite glory, he nevertheless remained the Son of God. The infinite and eternal God, the one from whom angels cover their eyes (Isa. 6:1–4), is, in fact, Jesus of Nazareth (John 12:41). Isaiah beheld the glory of Christ in a vision and was undone. God took on the form of a servant (Phil. 2:5–7), being born of a woman and under the law (Gal. 4:4–5). This Jesus, himself God, "the blessed and only Sovereign, the King of kings and Lord of lords, who alone has immortality, who dwells in unapproachable light" (1 Tim. 6:15–16), has condescended from his palace of exaltation to his place of humiliation (Phil. 2:5–8). Considering who we are and who he is, the fact that Christ says he's not ashamed to call us brothers has staggering implications.

Dear Christian, if you ever struggle to believe that God loves you, especially as you feel the weight of your weakness, remember that God became a man for you. To summarize Thomas Watson, it's a more extraordinary demonstration of humility for Christ to become a man than it is for him to die. It's natural for a man to die, but unheard of for God to become a man.[6] Far from Jesus being ashamed of his people, the fact that he became a man showcases his love for us.

His Suffering for Us

Jesus didn't back into the cross. His suffering and death for us was intentional and motivated by his eternal love. He willingly chose to come, live, and die for us and our salvation. His face was set like a flint to go and suffer (Isa. 50:7; Luke 9:51). He loved his own, even to the end (John 13:1). This love continued even onto the cross where Jesus prayed for those who opposed him and proclaimed the gospel to those who mocked him (Luke 23:34–43). Paul says that the cross was the supreme display of God's love for you:

> For while we were still weak, at the right time Christ died for the ungodly. For one will scarcely die for a righteous person— though perhaps for a good person one would dare even to die—but God shows his love for us in that while we were still sinners, Christ died for us. (Rom. 5:6–8)

Think of how rare it is for someone to sacrifice his life for a good person. But how much rarer is it to give one's life for an enemy

---

6 Thomas Watson, *The Christian's Charter of Privileges*, in vol. 1 of *Discourses on Important and Interesting Subjects, Being the Select Works of the Rev. Thomas Watson*, 2 vols. (Glasgow: Blackie, Fullarton, 1829), 1:128.

(Rom. 5:10)? This is meant to reassure us in moments of doubt and despair: "He who did not spare his own Son but gave him up for us all, how will he not also with him graciously give us all things?" (Rom. 8:32). This is an argument from the greater to the lesser. If God took care of your biggest problem, which cost him the most, how much more can you trust him to take care of your relatively minor problems? He's proven his love for you at the cross.

Besides being the most violent and torturous way to die, nothing was more soaked with shame than crucifixion—so much so that people considered it improper to even speak of crucifixion in polite company. The one crucified was nailed to the cross, completely naked, in the thoroughfare into the city so that all could see the power of the Romans. The victims were mocked by people and picked at by birds. It was horrible.

But in addition to this, when Jesus was on the cross, the sin of his people was charged to him, "For our sake he made him to be sin who knew no sin, so that in him we might become the righteousness of God" (2 Cor. 5:21). While physically naked, Jesus was swaddled in the garments of our sin. He publicly bore our shame, guilt, and curse.

The cross should settle the question of whether Jesus is ashamed of you. He endured such shame and suffering because he loves his people. It would be a great insult to question the love of one who went to such depths to display it.

God wants us to know that Jesus loved us before the cross, on the cross, and after the cross. I do hope you see the value of looking through Christ's eyes and sensing his love for you. He's not ashamed of his people.

John Owen writes of the value of reminding a believer that "God in Jesus Christ loves him, delights in him, is well pleased with him, has thoughts of tenderness and kindness toward him; to give, I say, a soul an overflowing sense thereof, is an inexpressible mercy."[7] When sitting under a shadow of depression, discouragement, or guilt that seems like it will never budge, remember this in that very moment: our Lord Christ is not ashamed to claim you as part of his family. He proved his love to you on the cross (Rom. 8:32). His sufferings console us. And remember, Christ's heart in heaven is the same toward us as it was when he was on earth. "He loved us then; he'll love us now."[8]

We would do our souls well to reflect on the eternal oath between the members of the Trinity, Christ's solidarity with us in the incarnation, and the extent of his sufferings for us. Indeed, he is not ashamed to call us brothers. Look at what he's said and done. Praise the Lord!

What I Aim to Do in This Book

In this book we will examine the types of people God delights to identify with. We'll see in chapter 1 that Jesus is not ashamed of those with an embarrassing history. Nobody has a story that can make Jesus blush. He doesn't Photoshop anyone out of the picture. In chapter 2, we'll look at some who opposed Jesus and yet were saved by him. Christ delights to showcase his mercy by turning his enemies into ambassadors. In chapter 3, we'll consider

7   John Owen, *Communion with the Triune God,* ed. Kelly Kapic and Justin Taylor (Wheaton, IL: Crossway, 2007), 378.

8   Dane Ortlund, *Gentle and Lowly: The Heart of Christ for Sinners and Sufferers* (Wheaton, IL: Crossway, 2020), 189. See 189–95.

how Jesus is not ashamed of those who are overlooked. Those who are marginalized by society have the eye of Jesus. In the fourth chapter, we'll think about those who were far from God. Jesus is not ashamed of them either; his mission is to seek and save the lost. In chapter 5, we'll look at the thief on the cross as an example of someone who has nothing to give Jesus. As we'll see, he is the perfect candidate for grace. In the sixth chapter, we'll think together about Jesus's choice to save those who are weak. In the seventh chapter, we'll see how the grace of Christ flows downhill to those who still sin. Jesus extends his nail-pierced hands to his children, who continue to hurt themselves and others. He is gracious indeed. In the final chapter, we'll see the only people whom Jesus is ashamed of—and it should strike us with sobering fear.

As we linger over the family photo of Jesus, we will be looking through the eyes of Christ to see the types of people his heart is drawn to. I pray that you would grow in your perception of God's staggering love and, in so doing, that you would have a greater sense of gratitude to and security in God. As you look at these snapshots of people whom God is not ashamed of, I hope you're reminded of the types of people he is drawn to, so that you would not stray far from his heart. Finally, I hope to testify of the unrivaled beauty of Jesus to those who are not yet following him. He is, in fact, just the Savior we need.

1

He Is Not Ashamed of Those with Embarrassing Stories

EVER MEET A TAMAR OR A RAHAB? Me neither. Why don't more people name their daughters Tamar or Rahab? Because they have shameful stories. Shame and embarrassment may be everyday experiences, but who would want to deliberately identify themselves with shame?

Embarrassment can result from something minor, like tripping over our own two feet in a crowded airport or accidentally belching during a presentation. The cause can also be more substantial and costly, like something said or done in private that unintentionally becomes known to others. It can arise from a deeply personal experience, either something that's happened to us or that we've done to others. Regardless of the circumstances, when we're embarrassed, we want to shrink and disappear. We want it—whatever *it* is—to go away.

Embarrassment sticks. We can feel awkward and ashamed before others, even if we're the only ones thinking about it. In those moments, our lives tell a story about us that we don't like. We're uncomfortably exposed. We'd rather tell a different narrative. We'd love another take.

Have you ever wanted a do-over? I have good news. There is someone willing to identify with people who have embarrassing stories and to remove the associated shame. He sympathizes with people who want to disappear. He's drawn to them. His heart is especially sensitive to those who are hurting. And he's seen everything (literally), so you can't make him blush. What's more, he is so powerful and so good that he's not only able to give us a second chance but also use our stories for good. Imagine that! Your worst nightmare can be used to make your dreams and longings come true.

Too good to be true? Hear me out. Turn to the opening verses of the New Testament and begin reading the genealogy of Jesus (Matt. 1:1–16).

No doubt some names are more familiar than others. Some surprise us. Double-click on a few names, and we find prostitutes, deceivers, and adulterers. Matthew breaks with his day's norms by including five women, most of them Gentiles, each with biographies that raise eyebrows. This is Jesus's family tree! Why would Matthew introduce his Gospel like this? Among other reasons, he means to convince us that Jesus is not ashamed of people with embarrassing stories. People with stories like Tamar, Rahab, Ruth, Bathsheba, and Mary are the types of people he sets his love on. They are his family.

In this chapter, I want to pull on the dangling thread of embarrassment and see how God has masterfully woven it into the tapestry of grace. We'll see how God brings comfort to the hurting. People in Jesus's family photo have shameful stories. I can't wait for you to meet them. You may find yourself relating to some of them.

Tamar, the Desperate Widow, Comes Home

And Judah the father of Perez and Zerah by Tamar. (Matt. 1:3)

The fourth name in Jesus's genealogy is Judah. He's Jacob's son and the father of Perez and Zerah. Judah figures prominently in the Genesis narrative and the development of the Old Testament. But neither Judah nor his sons catch our attention here. Tamar does. She's not even Judah's wife. She's actually his daughter-in-law. Confused? Unsettled? Before we untie this embarrassing knot, let's think about the context that leads up to their story.

Judah married a Canaanite woman, and they had three sons: Er, Onan, and Shelah. The oldest, Er, also married a Canaanite woman named Tamar. But he was put to death by the Lord for his wickedness (Gen. 38:7). Judah then told his unmarried second son, Onan, to fulfill his responsibility according to the custom[1] and have children with Tamar "to raise up offspring" for his brother (38:8). But Onan was wicked like his brother. He was happy to give the appearance of nobility by publicly taking Tamar as his wife, but he only used her to gratify himself sexually, refusing to give her a child (38:9). God judged Onan's selfishness and, like his brother, put him to death. When Judah took stock of the situation, he sent Tamar back to her father's house in Canaan.

---

1   In Deut. 25:5–6 the process for a Levirate marriage is outlined. From the Latin *levir,* meaning "husband's brother," the practice involves a childless widow marrying the nearest relative of her husband in order to provide an heir for the deceased.

Whether seeing her as a reminder of the painful stories of judgment or a bad-luck charm, he kicked her out of his house. She left Judah's house, the family of promise, with these embarrassing stories and the sense of being cursed looming over her head like a dark shadow. Why was it so crucial for Tamar to be married and have a child? This is a more significant cultural matter than most of us experience today. For Tamar to be married and have a child meant having a place. Without this, she was vulnerable and helpless. She desperately wanted to be in a house and hoped to have a child. But Judah sent her back to her father's house. He sent this member of his family back to Canaan. And so she left in search of a place. Adorned with mourning garments, Tamar, the widow, made the lonely walk to the wilderness, resembling one who bears the curse. Her only hope at this point was a thin promise from Judah: "Remain a widow in your father's house, till Shelah my son grows up" (Gen. 38:11).

Years later, Judah's wife died, and he went up to a sheep-shearing festival with some friends. These parties were known to be lively affairs as the shepherds sheared sheep and drank heavily.[2] Tamar found out that her father-in-law went to the festival and hatched a plan to go. We read, "She took off her widow's garments and covered herself with a veil, wrapping herself up, and sat at the entrance to Enaim, which is on the road to Timnah" (38:14). She took off her garments of mourning, customary attire for her as a widow, and put on a veil, which along with her decision to sit by the road, gave her the appearance of a prostitute. Why did

---

2 See 1 Sam. 25 when Nabal went to a similar festival and got roaring drunk. This is a key bit of information because the alcohol likely contributed to why Judah did not recognize Tamar.

she do this? Because Judah bailed on his promise. Judah's third son was grown up and was not given to her in marriage (38:14).

Hard to imagine this story becoming more cringeworthy, but it does.

> When Judah saw her, he thought she was a prostitute, for she had covered her face. He turned to her at the roadside and said, "Come, let me come in to you," for he did not know that she was his daughter-in-law. She said, "What will you give me, that you may come in to me?" (Gen. 38:15–16)

Judah was now propositioning his daughter-in-law for sex. He had no idea it was her, of course. The veil over her face, along with the generous amount of alcohol he'd likely imbibed at the festival, hid her identity from him. After quibbling about the amount and manner of payment, Judah agreed to give her his signet, cord, and staff as collateral. Like a modern-day wallet, all three of these items would quickly identify Judah.[3] And with shocking simplicity, we read, "So he gave them to her and went in to her, and she conceived by him. Then she arose and went away, and taking off her veil she put on the garments of her widowhood" (38:18–19). This is equal parts sad, embarrassing, and painful. Imagine this was how your mom got pregnant with you? A sense of embarrassment and shame like this lingers.

But this story is not over yet.

---

3 A signet was something that could be used on a ring or seal to make his mark, the chord likely hung around his neck, and the staff was an everyday tool used when walking. Any of Judah's family and friends, seeing these items, would know they were his.

In due time, Judah arranged for his friend to take payment to the woman whom he believed to be a prostitute, but the man couldn't find her.[4] Fearing embarrassment, Judah instructed his friend to forget it and let the woman keep his stuff. But shame would soon come to the house of Judah.

Three months later, the news spread that Tamar had been immoral and was now pregnant. As the news came to Judah, this philanderer suddenly transformed into an oak of righteous morality, sentencing his daughter-in-law to death. On her way to execution, Tamar had a word to share: "As she was being brought out, she sent word to her father-in-law, 'By the man to whom these belong, I am pregnant.' And she said, 'Please identify whose these are, the signet and the cord and the staff'" (38:25). The music stops. Every eye turns—glued on Judah. His heart thumping, Judah gulped and admitted the indicting evidence as his own. Judah's proud head dropped in shame, and he couldn't look anyone in the eye. He owned it: These are mine. The child is mine. Whatever you think of her, think less of me. "She is more righteous than I" (38:26). Shame had indeed come to Judah's house.

Throughout the story, the conflict surrounds Tamar's childlessness. She buried two wicked husbands, was duped by a tricky father-in-law, and seemed hopeless. But now she was pregnant with twins. God blesses the undeserving with abundance. Illustrating this point, the story concludes with an unusual birth. At the time of the birth, one son put out his hand, and the midwife tied the thread on it, pronouncing, "This one came out first" (38:28). Surprisingly, he drew his hand back, and his brother was born

---

4   This area, called Enaim, means "two eyes" and is ironically a place where people aren't able to see very clearly.

first—but was not the firstborn. That honor was for Perez: the one with the scarlet thread. This birth encapsulates a biblical truth: the underserving receive the blessing. Whether Perez, Tamar, Judah, or you and me—none of us deserve God's blessings but receive them wholly by his grace and kindness.

When Matthew includes Tamar, Judah, and their children's names in Jesus's genealogy, he means to make a point: Jesus comes from a line of people with messy, embarrassing, and shameful stories. And not only does he come *from* messy people, but he also comes *for* them. And as we'll see shortly, this has massive implications for how we understand our experiences and actions. Jesus isn't ashamed of you or your story. With Jesus, it's okay not to be okay. He has sufficient compassion and power to deal with you and me. We see this as the story continues.

Ruth, the Outcast, Draws Near

And Salmon the father of Boaz by Rahab, and Boaz the father of Obed by Ruth, and Obed the father of Jesse, and Jesse the father of David the king. And David was the father of Solomon by the wife of Uriah. (Matt. 1:5–6)

The book of Ruth is a tender story about devotion, redemption, and God's providence. A love story unexpectedly blossoms, turning tears of sorrow into tears of joy. But the book also makes some meaningful connections for us. As the genealogy in Matthew makes clear, the book of Ruth adds more faces to the family photo of Jesus. Considering the characters and their actions in Ruth, we find *lots of shame*. We also see one who's *not ashamed* because he loves.

The story of Ruth begins in the time of the judges (about 1100 BC), when hope seemed as scarce as food. Israel was a turbulent nation. If we took their spiritual temperature, they'd be ill. The final verse in the book of Judges reflects this: "In those days there was no king in Israel. Everyone did what was right in his own eyes" (Judg. 21:25). The opening verses of Ruth introduce us to a couple named Elimelech and Naomi, who were from the Messianic line of Judah (Ruth 1:1–2; Mic. 5:2). Though they were from Bethlehem, meaning "house of bread," their house lacked bread—they were living through a famine. A food shortage was often understood as God's judgment on the faithlessness of the covenant community (Lev. 26:23–26; Deut. 32:23–24). We are meant to sense the dark clouds of despair casting shadows on the tear-stained cheeks of this seemingly hopeless family.

The couple and their sons left Bethlehem searching for food and went to the other side of the Dead Sea, to Moab. "They went into the country of Moab and remained there" (Ruth 1:2). Additionally, we learn that the sons "took Moabite wives; the name of the one was Orpah and the name of the other Ruth. They lived there about ten years" (1:4). The family stayed in Moab, assimilating to the people and culture. During their time there, both Naomi's husband and her sons died.

There are contextual speedbumps to slow us down and give us a better view of where Ruth comes from. Knowing who the Moabites were helps us appreciate Boaz's kindness and the significance of Ruth's welcome into the royal line. When the Moabite train pulls into the family photo of Jesus, it brings cars and cars packed with unsettling, shocking, and embarrassing material. Let's pump the brakes and think about who the Moabites were.

To get the full Moabite story, we have to go back to their embarrassing beginning in Genesis with a man named Lot, the nephew of Abraham. And I warn you, the story isn't pretty.

Lot lived in Sodom, and God graciously warned him about Sodom's impending destruction (Gen. 19:12–22). Lot's family ran for their lives out of town. But while Lot and his daughters escaped, his wife looked back, becoming a pillar of salt (19:26). Standing in the pathway of deliverance, she became a monument of destruction. She reminds all to flee from the wrath of God and the folly of loving this world (Luke 17:28–32). With the odor of destruction still in their nostrils, Lot and his daughters retreated to Zoar, where they sought shelter in a cave. The cave may have been a suitable shelter, but soon it would become the setting for one of the most heinous scenes in all of the Bible.

After God's judgment of Sodom, Lot's daughters feared they wouldn't find a husband and have children. Their solution? Get dad drunk and then take advantage of him to become pregnant. On consecutive nights, they executed their sinful scheme. Lot got drunk with wine and got his daughters pregnant—yet another shameful story involving a woman deceiving a dishonorable man to have children. When we line up for the family photo, I'm guessing no one would want to stand next to Lot and his daughters.

Lot's daughters had two sons, and they became the Moabites and Ammonites. These two nations are not the good guys in biblical history. Due to their persistent opposition to Israel and rank idolatry, God excluded them from Israel's worship (Deut. 23:3–6). The Moabites and Ammonites were responsible for two of the most shocking monuments of rebellion in the Bible: the sin of Baal-Peor (Num. 25) and the worship of Molech, associated with child sacrifice (2 Kings 21:6; 2 Chron. 28:3). In fact, in back-to-back chapters, the prophet Jeremiah spells certain doom on these nations (the Moabites in Jer. 48 and the Ammonites in Jer. 49).[5]

Thus, going to Moab was going away from God. To identify with a Moabite was seen as shameful. And shame is what we find in the book of Ruth.

Ruth's widowed mother-in-law, Naomi, heard that the Lord had provided food for his people and decided to head home to Israel. Since she didn't have any more sons for them to marry, she sent away her daughters-in-law. But Ruth insisted on coming. She demonstrated remarkable loyalty to Naomi and faith in God, saying,

> Do not urge me to leave you or to return from following you. For where you go I will go, and where you lodge I will lodge. Your people shall be my people, and your God my God. Where you die I will die, and there will I be buried. May the LORD do so to me and more also if anything but death parts me from you. (Ruth 1:16–17)

Upon returning, Ruth went out to a field to glean some grain.[6] Boaz, the owner of the field, saw Ruth and asked about her. His men identified her by her hard work, manners, and heritage. But pay attention to how the man in charge of the crew replied to

---

5 This paragraph has been adapted from Erik Raymond, "The Christmas Present in Lot's Cave," *The Gospel Coalition*, December 12, 2016, https://www.thegospelcoalition.org/.

6 There is a gracious provision in the law permitting the poor, sojourners, orphans, and widows to gather grain from the four corners of the fields (Lev. 19:9–10).

Boaz, "She is the young Moabite woman" (2:6). Do you get the point? Ruth is a foreigner, even a Moabitess.

Boaz models God's love for people with embarrassing stories. Boaz helped the poor, widowed Moabitess. He identified with her and all of her baggage. He displayed extraordinary kindness to Ruth. Instead of being repelled by her, he drew near. He invited her to enjoy the better grain, his protection, and refreshment (2:8–16). Unexpectedly, Boaz was kind to Ruth. With total self-awareness and understanding of what it meant to be a Moabite in Israel, Ruth fell on her face and asked him, "Why have I found favor in your eyes, that you should take notice of me, since I am a foreigner?" (2:10). Yes, *why* would someone like Boaz help someone like Ruth? Why would he choose to identify with her when everyone else would not? Why would he choose to approach her shame?

Boaz answered, citing her kindness and faithfulness to Naomi. Also, he reminded her of her faith in God: "The LORD repay you for what you have done, and a full reward be given you by the LORD, the God of Israel, under whose wings you have come to take refuge!" (2:12).

Meanwhile, a light bulb went off in Naomi's mind. Boaz was a relative and an eligible redeemer.[7] Naomi planned for Ruth to go to Boaz's field at night and propose marriage to him! The plan unfolded with a scene rich in ancient culture, humility, love, and purity. Ruth laid at his feet as he slept. Upon waking at midnight, Boaz was shocked. In the darkness, she identified herself and explained, "I am Ruth, your servant. Spread your wings over your servant, for you are a redeemer" (3:9).

---

7   According to the Levirate marriage arrangement outlined in Deut. 25:5–6 and referenced in the Tamar narrative above.

In this bold proposal, Ruth took the words that Boaz used earlier and applied them to him. Boaz encouraged Ruth to take refuge under *God's wings* (2:12). But here, Ruth asked Boaz to spread *his wings* over her. Why? Ruth understood that God was the source of every blessing, and *Boaz was God's means* to bless her. God would take care of Ruth through Boaz. The plan to bring a foreigner home hatched under the midnight stars in Bethlehem.

There's a snag, though, with the plan. Legally, Boaz was not the closest relative. Another man in town was a more eligible redeemer. Boaz had to clear his intentions with this eligible relative. The next day, Boaz addressed the man. He informed him of the land that Naomi was selling and his eligibility to redeem it. The man heard of the opportunity to acquire the land and answered, "I will redeem it" (4:4). Boaz then included the detail that taking the land also meant taking Ruth the Moabitess. Hearing this, the man decided to pass on the offer (4:5–6). He was interested in the land but not in the daughter of Moab. Was it her shame that repelled him? He declined the offer and gave the right of redemption to Boaz. Dramatically, Boaz summarized the deal for the witnesses present:

> Then Boaz said to the elders and all the people, "You are witnesses this day that I have bought from the hand of Naomi all that belonged to Elimelech and all that belonged to Chilion and to Mahlon. Also Ruth the Moabite, the widow of Mahlon, I have bought to be my wife, to perpetuate the name of the dead in his inheritance, that the name of the dead may not be cut off from among his brothers and from the gate of his native place. You are witnesses this day." (Ruth 4:9–10)

The witnesses offered their best wishes for both Ruth and Boaz. To Ruth, they expressed a desire that God would be pleased to use her like Rachel and Leah to build up the house of Israel (4:11). To Boaz, they drew on the story of Perez.[8] In a short time, they married, and the Lord gave them a son. They named him Obed. He would be the grandfather of David, the king.

Why would someone like Boaz help someone like Ruth? Because God chose to love Ruth through Boaz, a redeemer. Through Boaz, God provided refuge and care to her (2:12; 3:9). God draws near to and cares for people like Ruth, a person who couldn't outrun the shadow of her family's history. But God eclipsed the shadow with the shining face of his covenant love. And then, he punctuates the point by listing Ruth in Jesus's genealogy. Jesus comes *from* people with embarrassing stories, and he also comes *for* them.

Conclusion

The stories of Tamar and Ruth are similar. Both are foreigners. Both have shameful stigmas associated with their names. And both figure prominently in the genealogy of Jesus.

But they're not the only ones. There's Rahab, the Canaanite prostitute who helped the spies in Israel (Josh. 2); Bathsheba, the widow of Uriah and the one with whom David committed adultery (2 Sam. 11); and Mary who, out of wedlock, miraculously conceived Jesus through the Holy Spirit (Luke 1:26–38). In each scandalous story, we find people in the family photo of Jesus that we wouldn't expect to see. If we were writing the

---

8 It was after Onan refused his right to redeem Tamar, that she became pregnant with Perez through Judah.

genealogy, we might have put different women in the list. But God doesn't do this. Instead, he highlights women with noteworthy scandals.

Why? To make this point: Jesus comes from messy people, and he comes for them. Jesus isn't ashamed of you or your story. Of course, not everything we've done is okay. This is why we need a Savior in the first place. But our shameful stories don't repel Jesus. He knows our shame, and he still loves us. In fact, it was his loving response to our guilt, sin, and shame that compelled him to come for us (John 3:16). He is drawn to us in our guilt. He identifies with us in our shame. Even the circumstances of Jesus's birth underscore this. Our Lord's mother, Mary, was assumed to be guilty of scandalous sin when she miraculously became pregnant (Matt. 1:18–19). This stigma likely followed Jesus his whole life (see John 8:41). He came into the world with suspicions of scandal in his immediate family and confirmed cases in his family tree. Then on the cross, Jesus became sin for us (2 Cor. 5:21). As the hymn writer says,

> Bearing shame and scoffing rude,
> In my place condemned he stood.[9]

His whole point in coming was to identify with us and deal with our shame. He's not ashamed to call people like us his family.

So many people carry around the embarrassment, shame, and pain from their experiences. Jesus's genealogy shows us that Christ brings hope and healing. Glance again at the family photo

---

9 Philip P. Bliss, "Hallelujah! What a Savior!," 1875.

of Jesus. Think about the implications of this for yourself and the people you know.

- Like Tamar, have you been sexually mistreated—or even sexually abused?
- Like Ruth, have you experienced the biting sting of racism?
- Like Judah, have you oppressed and victimized others?
- Like Perez, or even Jesus, were you born out of wedlock?
- Like Tamar, and even Mary, have you conceived children out of wedlock?
- Like Judah, Rahab, and David, have you been sexually immoral?
- Like Tamar, have you been rejected by your family?

No matter how shameful, embarrassing, or painful your experiences feel to you or appear to others, remember that nothing can extinguish Christ's redemptive love for his people. Jesus comes in the line of David, with Moabite and Canaanite blood in his veins. He came from people with shameful stories, and he came for them. This must be a source of comfort, joy, and gratitude for us every day. Scan the faces in the family photo of Jesus and see those whose stories did not repel Christ's heart. Many may be tempted to airbrush them out, but look again. He's standing there among them. Rising above the commotion of painful memories from your past, dear Christian believer, Jesus's voice speaks to you: "I am not ashamed of you. You are part of my family. I love you."

2

He Is Not Ashamed of Those
Who Opposed Him

"ONCE YOUR ENEMY, now seated at Your table, Jesus, thank You."[1] These words punctuate the chorus of a familiar hymn sung in many churches. As you read these words, which part is more difficult to believe? The fact that you were once an enemy or that in Christ, you are welcome, like family, at God's table? It depends on how you see yourself and how you think God sees you.

Were we really enemies of God? And, if so, does God indeed welcome us in the most intimate setting of fellowship with him? I think so. The song gets it right. And when we understand this, then things begin to change for us. When we know what we deserve and what God gives us instead, we start to experience increasing gratitude, humility, security, and evangelistic zeal. God is not ashamed of welcoming and identifying with his former enemies. Such people stand out as monuments of his grace.

1 Pat Sczebel, "Jesus, Thank You," Sovereign Grace Music, https://sovereigngracemusic.org/.

Theological Framework

Minimizing sin has a dangerous side-effect. It minimizes grace. By downplaying how lost we were, we run the risk of underappreciating how staggering the rescue is. It's one thing for me to tell you that I got lost in a shopping mall and couldn't find the way back to where I parked. But it's quite another matter to be lost in the mountains of Colorado before being dramatically recovered by a mountain rescue unit. When thinking about how sin separates us from God, we have to be clear on the degree of the problem. Otherwise, we risk downgrading the gospel to a friendly volunteer at a kiosk giving directions rather than a breathtaking rescue mission.

The biblical teaching is clear, "All have sinned and fall short of the glory of God" (Rom. 3:23). Every single person who has ever lived, except for the Lord Jesus, has sinned. A sin is a violation of God's word (1 John 3:4), either by failing to do what God says or by doing what God says not to do. But that's not all. Our natural disposition is opposition to God. We were born into this fallen state of rebellion. All of us are "by nature children of wrath" (Eph. 2:3). And this fallen state leads to sinful actions. Sin and separation from God don't lie dormant. Sin is active. Therefore, all people are sinners both by nature and by choice.

The language the Bible uses to describe people in their unconverted state can be jolting. I think that's the point. The words are meant to rattle us. Some of the descriptions of unbelievers include "wicked" (Ps. 10:3); "a slave to sin" (John 8:34); "full of envy, murder, strife, deceit, maliciousness" (Rom 1:29); "haters of God" (Rom. 1:30); "inventors of evil" (Rom. 1:30); "enemies" (Rom. 5:10); "hostile to God" (Rom. 8:7); "evil" (2 Thess. 3:2);

and "foolish" (Titus 3:3). This language doesn't reflect ambivalence but rather active opposition to God. In terms of our status before God, we are all sinners, but the degree of expression may differ. As Spurgeon says, "They are all in the mire; but they have not all sunk to an equal depth in it."[2] While some people's sins may be more pronounced than others, all people—even you and me—-stand naturally opposed to God.

In a summary form, the apostle Paul writes that we "once were alienated and hostile in mind, doing evil deeds" (Col. 1:21). You can see the progression here. Alienation refers to a status; by nature we are separated from God. Hostility in mind is a mind at war with God. This translates into the action Paul labels as "evil deeds." Even though he hadn't met the Christians in Colossae and the surrounding regions (2:1), Paul confidently labels them this way. How could he do this without knowing them personally, without sizing them up morally? Because this is the common condition for all people. Our natural state is helplessly and hopelessly depraved. This is what it means to be lost.

But God acts. He pursues us. He rescues the rebels. Those who were enemies are reconciled through the death of Christ (1:21–22). Those who were alienated, hostile in mind, and doing evil deeds are now reconciled to God. And one day they will be presented "holy, blameless, and above reproach before him" (1:22).

Now and then, we come across a scene in a book, in a film, or in the news that reflects this type of radical reconciliation. And when we do, it shakes us and brings with it a mandatory moment of silence. One example came in a courtroom in 2019. After an

2   C. H. Spurgeon, "A Great Gospel for Great Sinners," in *The Metropolitan Tabernacle Pulpit Sermons* (London: Passmore & Alabaster, 1885), 31:231.

off-duty police officer killed his brother, Brandt Jean was allowed to give a victim impact statement. He addressed Amber Guyger, the woman who shot his brother:

> If you truly are sorry, I can speak for myself, I forgive, and I know if you go to God and ask him, he will forgive you. And I don't think anyone can say it—again I'm speaking for myself—but I love you just like anyone else. And I'm not gonna say I hope you rot and die just like my brother did, but I presently want the best for you.[3]

Then he asked the judge if he could hug Ms. Guyger. The judge permitted, and the image of a grieving, yet forgiving, brother hugging the woman who took his brother's life flooded the news. It challenged the limits of forgiveness and the possibility of reconciliation. To forgive and embrace someone who caused such pain is not common. It's extraordinary. It's shocking grace.

Yet, as riveting as this scene was, our reconciliation to God is ratcheted up a few levels. Our crimes against God are even more heinous because God is so holy. And while people commonly show remorse for the *consequences* of sin, remorse is rarely expressed for the sinfulness of the sin itself. We hate how sin makes us feel. We fear sin's repercussions or its punishments in this life, but we do not hate how it dishonors God. Looking through the lenses of God's infinite holiness and our sin's ugliness, we begin to better appreciate God moving toward his enemies with the embrace of

---

3 Ashley Killough, Darran Simon, and Ed Lavandera, "His Hug of Forgiveness Shocked the Country. Yet He Still Won't Watch the Video from That Moment," CNN, December 8, 2019, https://www.cnn.com/.

the gospel. By means of his grace, he says, "I love you. I forgive you. I want you to be part of my family."

Think again about the above-quoted song lyrics: "Once Your enemy, now seated at Your table, Jesus, thank You." Perhaps you see more clearly the depth of our alienation from God and the loving grace that sets your place at the family table. But if you're like me, then you're prone to forget this, especially when you sin or remember things you've done. This is why it's good to see through the eyes of Christ and understand how he looks at those who opposed him. He's not ashamed of them. Instead, he loves them. He delights in conquering them with his grace and in welcoming them to his feast. Let me show you a couple of biblical examples to make my point and, in doing so, encourage you about the significance and security of the believer's position in Christ.

Go to Jerusalem

After his resurrection and before his ascension to heaven, Jesus commissioned his disciples to take the gospel to the ends of the earth (Matt. 28:19–20). He intended this small group of followers to faithfully multiply themselves by proclaiming the message of his life, death, burial, and resurrection. It's noteworthy that Luke twice emphasizes that this mission was to begin in Jerusalem (Luke 24:47; Acts 1:8). Preach the gospel, Jesus said, to all nations, but begin in Jerusalem. Why? There are many possible answers, but I want to focus on one. Jesus vectored his evangelists to Jerusalem because he delights to save big sinners. He loves to save those who opposed him.

The Jerusalem of Jesus's day was familiar to him. He spent a lot of time there proclaiming the gospel of the kingdom of God. He shed tears over the city even as he endured its hostility. Ultimately, the leaders of the town rejected, mocked, and delivered him up to death. They committed an infinite crime by killing the one who was altogether lovely and good. What city in history could rival such wickedness? Yet Jesus wanted his disciples to begin their ministry in the town that killed him and to plant a church in the shadow of the cross. In this way, Jesus demonstrated that he loves to save the biggest sinners. His heart is directed in mercy toward those who opposed him with venom.

John Bunyan reflected on how surprising this is to consider, since it was only a few weeks prior that these people in Jerusalem "had their hands up to the elbows in his heart's blood."[4] He could've sent his disciples to the rest of the world first and then, perhaps, come back to Jerusalem. That still would've been grace—remarkable grace. But what can we call this grace that pivots out of the empty tomb to deputize his evangelists to proclaim the gospel first to those who killed him?

Jesus Christ is the Savior of sinners. And he dispatched his disciples to Jerusalem, "the city that kills the prophets and stones those who are sent to it" (Matt. 23:37), prioritizing the most notable sinners in his lifetime. In the true economy of the gospel, he gave the cream to those who seem the least deserving. The firstfruits in the barn of salvation would be among the most surprising.

This is exactly what his disciples did. The book of Acts unfolds like a perfectly executed game plan. In chapter 2, Peter stood up to preach and didn't mince words. He laid out the details of their sin:

4 John Bunyan, *The Jerusalem Sinner Saved*, in *The Works of John Bunyan*, ed. George Offor, 3 vols. (Edinburgh: Banner of Truth Trust, 1991), 1:71.

Men of Israel, hear these words: Jesus of Nazareth, a man attested to you by God with mighty works and wonders and signs that God did through him in your midst, as you yourselves know—this Jesus, delivered up according to the definite plan and foreknowledge of God, you crucified and killed by the hands of lawless men. (Acts 2:22–23)

Peter explained how they were guilty of killing the Messiah. He quoted Psalm 110, calling *them* the enemies of God (Acts 2:34–35; cf. Ps. 110:1). Think how unpalatable this would have been to these proud Israelites. But Peter wanted them to know the truth. God was on Jesus's side, and by virtue of their crime, he was not on theirs. And stunningly, the people responded with contrition. God the Holy Spirit attended Peter's preaching with his power. Those who formerly rejected Christ now were crying out under intense conviction.

Now when they heard this they were cut to the heart, and said to Peter and the rest of the apostles, "Brothers, what shall we do?" And Peter said to them, "Repent and be baptized every one of you in the name of Jesus Christ for the forgiveness of your sins, and you will receive the gift of the Holy Spirit. For the promise is for you and for your children and for all who are far off, everyone whom the Lord our God calls to himself." (Acts 2:37–39)

Christ started winning his trophies of grace in Jerusalem. He pursued those who opposed him because he wanted them to be part of his family. They hated him, but he loved them. Luke writes,

"So those who received his word were baptized, and there were added that day about three thousand souls" (Acts 2:41). Mercy conquered three thousand enemies! See how willing Christ is to win murderers with the word of life! Once his enemies, now we are seated at his table.

Consider this scene and see through the eyes of Christ. He is not ashamed to identify with those who've opposed him. You can imagine the objections that would've welled up in the hearers' hearts and how the gospel answered their deepest concerns.[5]

Objection: "But I plotted for him to be killed. How can I be saved?"
Answer: "The promise is for you."

Objection: "But I bore false witness against him. Is there grace for me?"
Answer: "There is grace for you from the King of grace."

Objection: "But I cried out, 'Crucify him, crucify him'; and desired that Barabbas, the murderer, might live, rather than *him*."
Answer: "Repent and be baptized every one of you!"

Objection: "But I spit in his face and mocked him."
Answer: "Though you were ashamed of him, he won't be of you."

5   Adapted from Bunyan, *The Jerusalem Sinner Saved*, 1:72.

Objection: "But I rejoiced when I thought he was defeated. Is there any hope for me?"

Answer: "There is hope for every one of you who call on the name of the Lord."

This is a sample of the types of people who are part of Christ's family. It's no accident that these events took place on the day of Pentecost. This was one of the great annual feasts in Israel, celebrated seven weeks after Passover. It's also called the Feast of Harvest (Ex. 23:16) and the day of the firstfruits (Num. 28:26) because the initial part of the harvest was gathered in.

In Acts 2, we have the firstfruits of the church's harvest. As these souls are gathered into the barn of grace, they indicate the types of people that Jesus is pleased to identify with. On the Feast of Harvest, new people are added to the family photo of Jesus. Those who were his enemies are now welcomed at his table.

Paul, the Chief of Sinners

When we think about the love of Christ toward those who opposed him, there is perhaps no more familiar example than the apostle Paul. This is quite a story: the man who went to arrest Christians got arrested by Christ. We must be careful to keep the proper point of reference in focus as we think about this. The story is not primarily about how bad Paul was but how good God is. His alienation from God shows us how far the train of mercy will travel to pick up its passengers. Later, when reflecting on his conversion, Paul reminds his readers that it should serve as an example for others. If Saul of Tarsus, the chief of sinners ("the foremost" sinner; see 1 Tim. 1:15), the archenemy of the Lord, can find mercy, then who is too bad to be saved?

In the New Testament, Paul is known by his Hebrew name, Saul, until Acts 13:9. He was a well-trained Pharisee with unrivaled zeal, obedience, and esteem (Acts 22:3; Gal. 1:14; Phil. 3:5–6). This zeal translated into a ferocious desire to destroy the church (Gal. 1:13). As Stephen the faithful martyr for Christ testified of his faith, Saul stood by approving of the mob's sentence of death (Acts 8:1). But he wasn't content with snuffing out this one flame of faith: "Saul was ravaging the church, and entering house after house, he dragged off men and women and committed them to prison" (8:3). The word translated here as "ravaging" can be used to describe wild beasts tearing apart the flesh of their prey. When describing people's actions, it has the idea of destroying. When we consider the story of Saul of Tarsus, we should see a religious fanatic filled with anger, mercilessly ripping through the town, tearing men and women out of their houses and dragging them into prison.

In Acts 9:1–2, Luke shows how Saul intended to expand this persecution 150 miles north of Jerusalem to Damascus. Notice the intensity of Luke's words. Saul wanted to extinguish any flame of Christianity wherever he found it. "But Saul, still breathing threats and murder against the disciples of the Lord, went to the high priest and asked him for letters to the synagogues at Damascus, so that if he found any belonging to the Way, men or women, he might bring them bound to Jerusalem." In his own words, he would later write,

I persecuted this Way to the death, binding and delivering to prison both men and women (Acts 22:4)

And I did so in Jerusalem. I not only locked up many of the saints in prison after receiving authority from the chief priests, but when they were put to death I cast my vote against them. And I punished them often in all the synagogues and tried to make them blaspheme, and in raging fury against them I persecuted them even to foreign cities. (26:10–11)

Saul Meets Jesus

At this point in the story, the last thing anyone is rooting for is mercy. Instead, we naturally want justice. We want Saul to get what's coming to him. But that's not what happens. In an unexpected twist, the hunter becomes the hunted.[6]

Making his way along the seven-day journey to Damascus, armed with letters of extradition, he was startled by a noonday light from heaven that was brighter than the sun (Acts 22:6; 26:13). He fell to the ground and a voice from heaven said, "Saul, Saul, why are you persecuting me?" (26:14). Confused and no doubt greatly unnerved, he answered, "Who are you, Lord?"[7] Then came the answer, "I am Jesus, whom you are persecuting" (26:15).

Let's press pause on this scene for a minute and consider a question. In what sense was Saul persecuting Jesus? After all, Jesus had been resurrected and ascended to heaven. How could Saul affect him? The answer lies in Saul's persecution against his family, the church, the body of Christ. Jesus is the head of the church. He's closely identified with and connected to his people. If someone

---

6   R. Kent Hughes, *Acts: The Church Afire,* Preaching the Word (Wheaton, IL: Crossway, 1996), 126.

7   This is more likely an expression of submission to an unsettling display of transcendent power than an actual profession of faith at this point.

attacks the arm, then they attack the head also, for we are one body. John Stott observes, "At once Saul must have grasped, from the extraordinary way in which Jesus identified with his followers, so that to persecute them was to persecute him, that Jesus was alive and his claims were true."[8] Jesus is the exalted King of kings, but he's also a compassionate high-priest who sees and sympathizes with us in our weakness (Heb. 4:15). Dear Christian, you may feel alone at times, but you never escape the omnipresent eyes of your loving Savior.

In a moment, the wild wolf came face-to-face with the good shepherd of the flock of God. Here we see Jesus's power as King and his love as Savior. He is the one who delights to save his enemies and welcome them into his family. Here on the road to Damascus, the man intent on arresting Christians was arrested by Christ. This raging rebel and enemy of God was subdued by omnipotence and tamed by mercy. While the light from heaven blinded his eyes, mercy melted his heart. Reflecting on this verse, John Newton writes,

> If thou hadst bid thy thunders roll,
> And lightnings flash, to blast my soul,
> I still had stubborn been:
> But mercy has my heart subdu'd,
> A bleeding Saviour I have view'd
> And now I hate my sin.[9]

---

8 John R. W. Stott, *The Message of Acts: The Spirit, the Church & the World,* The Bible Speaks Today (Leicester, England; Downers Grove, IL: InterVarsity Press, 1994), 170.

9 John Newton, *The Works of John Newton,* 6 vols. (London: Hamilton, Adams, 1824), 3:440.

This experience that Paul had with the resurrected Lord shaped so much of what we read from him in the New Testament. If Jesus rose from the dead, then everything he said is true. It's that simple. He is God, worthy of unrivaled devotion, honor, and glory. The Prince of Peace is willing to forgive the chief of sinners.

Welcome Home

Jesus was not content simply to save a sinner like Saul, similar to those converted in Jerusalem earlier in Acts. He wanted to welcome Saul into his family and let him serve. In Saul's case, the shepherd tamed the wolf and put him in charge of the sheep. Jesus uses people who opposed his kingdom to now expand it. Jesus said to Saul, "But rise and enter the city, and you will be told what you are to do" (Acts 9:6). From there, Saul was led by the hand into Damascus. Although he was physically blind, he could see better than he ever could before.

At the same time, the Lord was preparing the disciples to receive Saul. The Lord appeared to a man named Ananias and instructed him to meet Saul to restore his eyesight (9:10–12). Now we need to remember that Saul of Tarsus was likely a household name at the time. His reputation of rage against the church had spread to Damascus. We can understand his response to the Lord's command: "But Ananias answered, 'Lord, I have heard from many about this man, how much evil he has done to your saints at Jerusalem. And here he has authority from the chief priests to bind all who call on your name'" (9:13–14).

But the Lord made it clear. Saul was part of the family now: "The Lord said to him, 'Go, for he is a chosen instrument of mine to carry my name before the Gentiles and kings and the children of Israel'" (9:15).

Ananias did as he was commanded. He met Saul, laid hands on him, and then Saul received his sight (9:17–18). But this was more than mere physical healing. This demonstrates how Christ welcomes people, even those who opposed him, into his family.

When Ananias heard that Saul was a "chosen instrument" in the Redeemer's hands, his perception of him changed. There are three sizable indicators that point to the enveloping of Saul into the body of Christ.

First, when Ananias met Saul, he called him "brother." He welcomed him into the family. Imagine that scene. It's hard to envision Ananias greeting him without a lump in his throat and tears in his eyes. The man he feared now stands before him as a brother.

Second, Saul was given the Holy Spirit. The promise of Christ to give the Holy Spirit to all of his followers had been fulfilled in Saul. God came to indwell Saul as one who had been made alive by the Spirit.

Finally, he was baptized. He publicly identified with Jesus and his people. He was welcomed into the church. Jesus's people affirmed on earth what was said in heaven; Saul was now a follower of Jesus. They were not ashamed to call him "brother" because Jesus was not ashamed of him. Even though he opposed Christ vehemently, he was welcomed into his new family. "Once Your enemy, now seated at Your table, Jesus, thank You."

Some Implications

Since every person is naturally born with the status of an enemy of God, everyone can relate in some way to these stories of opposition. Though our experiences and sins may be different, nevertheless, our standing apart from Christ is the same. Therefore, it is good for our souls to revisit these examples of how Jesus prioritizes and pursues his enemies. Consider these brief reflections in closing.

Jesus delights to save his enemies. Everything Christ does, he does for the glory of God. The plucking of one sinner from the path of destruction ignites a chorus of rejoicing in heaven (Luke 15:10). If you have come to Christ, you must know that heaven—even the Prince of heaven—rejoices.

Those who oppose God are prospects for grace. We might be tempted to write off certain people as too far from God. But is this true? What does the family photo of Jesus teach us? To paraphrase John Newton, none are so bad that the gospel cannot be their ground for hope, and none are so good as to have any hope without it.[10] Consider Stephen. The crowd responded to his faithful proclamation of the gospel by pelting him with rocks. How did he respond to that? In his last breaths, he prayed for them, "And falling to his knees he cried out with a loud voice, 'Lord, do not hold this sin against them.' And when he had said this, he fell asleep" (Acts 7:60). Don't forget that Saul of Tarsus was a member of that violent mob. The Lord answered Stephen's dying prayer. Our Lord can cure man's arrogance. He can lead a man to the knowledge of the evils of his heart.[11] May God help us to pray, preach, and share the gospel like we believe that God delights to save his enemies.

10 Newton, *Works*, 2:278.
11 Thomas Boston, *The Whole Works of Thomas Boston*, ed. Samuel M'Millan, 12 vols. (Aberdeen: George and Robert King, 1849), 4:369.

Our history does not eclipse our status. Paul was a bad guy; there is no doubt. But his past didn't hang over him. God made him a new person and used him significantly. His former life never defined him but only served as an encouraging example of the kind of mercy people who come to Jesus should expect to receive. In Philippians 3, Paul looks back to who he was (Phil. 3:4–6). Then he reminds himself and his readers of the privilege of the grace of Christ (3:7–10). And then he writes words that should be especially precious to those who formerly lived in active opposition to Christ, "Brothers, I do not consider that I have made it my own. But one thing I do: forgetting what lies behind and straining forward to what lies ahead, I press on toward the goal for the prize of the upward call of God in Christ Jesus" (3:13–14). Even though Paul, you, and I were formerly enemies of God, as soon as we come to Christ, we are welcomed at his table. We forget what lies behind, and we press on toward the goal. With our minds set on the loveliness of Christ (4:8), we go out, just as he has sent us, to call others home.

Could you imagine how our churches might change if we looked at people the way Jesus does?

3

He Is Not Ashamed of Those Who Are Overlooked

WHAT CATCHES YOUR EYE?

We tend to be attracted to things that we desire. We notice and pursue what we value. We might say, *out of the overflow of the heart, the eyes seek.*

What do people esteem today? I live in Metro Boston, where education is highly regarded. In New York City, people value the financial industry. In Washington D.C., political power dominates the conversation. In Los Angeles, the entertainment industry holds sway. More broadly, especially in the West, if someone has any combination of wealth, success, or physical attractiveness, then they likely enjoy some degree of influence. Status turns heads. It catches our eye. Influential people like this are esteemed.

This means that for the majority of us, we're on the outside looking in. Let's be honest. We're just ordinary, everyday people. Others walk by us on the sidewalk without a double take. Except by our family, friends, and co-workers, we're easily overlooked. What's so ironic is that we often look to those who have status and influence to give us meaning and purpose. We want to be like them—usually because we want acceptance. We want a place to belong. We want our lives to count and have value. We don't want to be overlooked.

In light of this, it's interesting to study the people Jesus noticed. As we consider this, we must remember that he's God. The implications of this truth are myriad. He needs nothing and owns everything. Nothing exists apart from him (Col. 1:16). Also, he has the highest honor. "He is the radiance of the glory of God" (Heb. 1:3). He has infinite riches, value, glory, and power. He has it all. He stands out. But who do we find him drawn to in his earthly ministry? Throughout his life, we see that his heart was inclined toward others who were easily overlooked. He was drawn to people who didn't usually turn heads.

This chapter will look at three categories of people that drew Jesus's attention: children, women, and the disabled. As we consider them, remember that Jesus never changes. Therefore, his heart in heaven remains like it was on earth. Those overlooked by many are not overlooked by him.

"Let the Children Come to Me"

In the first century, children were regarded as the least important members of society. They did not have any inherent status or power. The treatment of children fluctuated depending on how they might benefit their family. "Roman law gave the father absolute power (*patria potestas*) over his family—which extended to life and death. As late as A.D. 60, a son was put to death by the simple order of his father."[1] It's not hard to imagine the harshness and cruelty that could occur in this environment.

The Israelites lived within this cultural atmosphere. Inasmuch as their perspective of children was shaped by the Scriptures, it was quite different. They knew that children were created in the image of God (Gen. 1:26–27), knitted together in their mother's womb (Ps. 139:13), and given by God as a gift (Ps. 127:3). Children held inherent dignity and status because of their relationship to the Lord. God knew them, made them, and loved them. Children mattered. But, as is sadly often the case, even in our present day, one's biblical worldview can be corrupted by the surrounding unbelieving world. Like walking down a muddy path, you have to take care not to get soiled by your environment.

We find the tension between these two worldviews exposed in the Gospel narratives. In Mark 10:13, we read, "And they were bringing children to him that he might touch them." Among the Jewish people, there was a custom of bringing children to great men to receive a blessing. This goes back at least to the time of Jacob when he blessed his sons and grandsons before his death (Gen. 48). Because of his unprecedented ministry and influence, a sizable crowd of people had now emerged before Jesus. You can imagine the scene of parents assembling with eyes and hearts full of anticipation, carrying their cooing and drooling children, waiting for the Lord to put his hands on their heads.

The disciples of Jesus responded to this scene with a rebuke (Mark 10:13). We're not given the reason for their actions. Still, we wouldn't be wandering too far out on a limb to suggest that

---

1   R. Kent Hughes, *Mark: Jesus, Servant and Savior*, Preaching the Word (Westchester, IL: Crossway, 1989), 54–55.

they considered the children an unnecessary interruption in Jesus's day. We might even assume that their motives were commendable. They were probably trying to help Jesus.

The disciples' harsh rebuke of the parents may have been rude, but it was not necessarily a shock in its first-century context. Instead, Jesus's response gets our attention. The disciples' insensitivity provides an opportunity for us to see Christ's heart. As Charles Spurgeon observes about the disciples, "They thought them too little, too insignificant, and that the Master had greater things to do; but he thinketh not so."[2] The disciples saw the children as insignificant, but *he thinketh not so.*

Jesus's response should get our attention. We read, "But when Jesus saw it, he was indignant and said to them, 'Let the children come to me; do not hinder them, for to such belongs the kingdom of God'" (Mark 10:14). Who did Jesus direct his anger toward? His disciples. He rebuked the rebukers.[3] Why? Because they had obstructed the children. The disciples had shelved Jesus's previous lesson about children (see 9:36–37) in favor of convenience. They exhibited a worldly reflex that eclipsed a biblical priority. They overlooked those whom they deemed less significant. But, surprisingly, *he thinketh not so.*

We can learn a lot about people based on what angers them. Here we have a window into the heart of Christ. He has compassion for those who are weak. He defends the helpless. He stands up for the voiceless. He embraces the marginalized. His disciples

---

2   C. H. Spurgeon, "The Saviour's Charity," in *The Metropolitan Tabernacle Pulpit Sermons* (London: Passmore & Alabaster, 1915), 61:609.

3   Ben Witherington III, *The Gospel of Mark: A Socio-Rhetorical Commentary* (Grand Rapids, MI: Eerdmans, 2001), 279.

erected a barricade, but he tore it down. He clears the road of opposition and paves it with an invitation: "Let them come to me; do not hinder them." Invite them and do not prevent them.

Punctuating the statement, so that no one could misunderstand his point, Jesus "took them in his arms and blessed them, laying his hands on them" (10:16). You can imagine how the scene changed. In an instant, at the words and actions of Christ, the parents were relieved of feelings of rejection, disappointment, and insignificance. The children in their arms were not inconvenient or unimportant. They don't get in the way. In Jesus's eyes, they have dignity, value, and significance. Previously overlooked, they occupied center stage as an object lesson for the type of person that will enter the kingdom of God. The Lord rebuked a worldly philosophy that diminished children, while affirming their inherent value as divine image bearers. In that most riveting scene, we see the heart of Christ on display. He moves toward the marginalized. He loves the seemingly unimportant. With the rebuke of carnal men still ringing in their ears, these parents felt the heartbeat of Christ as he embraced their children. And we see a picture we should not soon forget, for, in due time, through his suffering upon the cross, the arms and hands of Jesus would again be a conduit of blessing to all who become like children and receive the kingdom of God.

"And Also Some Women"

When reading the Gospel accounts of the life and ministry of Jesus, a keen eye will note quite a few women written into the story. Just glance at the high points of Jesus's birth (Luke 1:26–56), death on the cross (23:49, 55–56), and resurrection

(Matt. 28:1–10), and you'll see women as prominent figures. Also, women appear at the center of many of Jesus's teaching illustrations (e.g., Luke 15:8–10; 18:1–8; 21:1–4) and as recipients of several important healings (e.g., 4:38–39; 8:43–48; 13:10–17). Today Jesus's treatment of women may hardly raise an eyebrow, but in the male-dominated culture of the first century, it would've surprised many.[4]

But isn't this what we'd expect to see if Jesus is the Savior of the whole world—of both men and women? In a world where people are trying to make their mark, Jesus came to make a mark on others. He came to make a new family in which people's identity is derived from their acceptance by God rather than from other people. These cultural realities of a bygone age serve as suitable backgrounds on which to paint the beautiful portrait of grace. Whether his actions are deemed politically correct or not today, Jesus was not ashamed of any of his followers.

One of those scenes that gets our attention occurs in Luke's Gospel.

Soon afterward he went on through cities and villages, proclaiming and bringing the good news of the kingdom of God. And the twelve were with him, and also some women who had been healed of evil spirits and infirmities: Mary, called Magdalene, from whom seven demons had gone out, and Joanna, the wife of Chuza, Herod's household manager, and Susanna, and many others, who provided for them out of their means. (Luke 8:1–3)

4   See Rebecca McLaughlin, *Confronting Christianity: 12 Hard Questions for the World's Largest Religion* (Wheaton, IL: Crossway, 2019), 131–52.

During his itinerant ministry of preaching the gospel, Jesus was accompanied by his disciples. But in this small group, we also have "some women." Women traveling with rabbis in ancient Israel was uncommon, so Luke's inclusion of this fact indicates that something unexpected was happening. Jesus broke with traditional norms to identify with people that others tended to overlook. He invited those whom others would not. Clearly, Jesus is different. And as we'll see, it's a refreshing difference.

Drilling down a bit into the text, we observe something further: women were recipients of the power, love, and grace of Christ. Luke points out that "some had been healed of evil spirits and infirmities," and then he cites examples: Mary Magdalene, Joanna, Susanna, and many others. There was nothing scandalous about their situation before they met Jesus; they were simply hurting and afflicted. In particular, Luke notes that Mary Magdalene was tormented by seven demons from which Jesus rescued her. These women were "Christ's patients" and "the monuments of his power and mercy."[5] Whether they had suffered from sickness, disease, or even demon possession, these precious disciples were now billboards for the glory of Christ. Their lives broadcast Jesus's love for them and power in them. Commenting on this text, John Calvin perceptively writes, "This enables us more clearly to perceive that the crimes with which we were loaded before we believed, are so far from diminishing the glory of Christ, that they tend rather to raise it to a higher pitch."[6] Jesus is not ashamed to identify with

---

5   Matthew Henry, *Matthew Henry's Commentary on the Whole Bible: Complete and Unabridged in One Volume* (Peabody, MA: Hendrickson, 1994), 1848.

6   John Calvin, *Commentary on a Harmony of the Evangelists Matthew, Mark, and Luke*, trans. William Pringle, 3 vols. (Bellingham, WA: Logos Bible Software, 2010), 2:99.

us because our dark circumstances prior to conversion do not dim but rather brighten our perception of his glory. Like a black velvet background enhancing the beauty of a sparkling diamond, our weakness and sin only serve to accentuate the various nuances of God's grace and love to us in Christ.

Additionally, notice Jesus's heart in motion during his ongoing public identification with them. He didn't simply heal or help them. No, he continued with them—and they with him. In fact, Jesus was so tied to this group of female disciples that they "provided for him out of their means" (Luke 8:3). Jesus was not only comfortable giving to them but also receiving from them. Consider the following examples, from Luke's Gospel, of women serving Jesus in his earthly ministry:

- Mary the mother of Jesus (1:26–38)
- A sinful woman washing his feet (7:36–49)
- Martha and Mary (10:38–42)
- Women at the crucifixion (23:49, 55–56)
- Women at the tomb (24:10–11)
- Women reporting the empty tomb (24:22–24)

Many of these snapshots of faithful service to Christ communicate the closeness of deep love and devotion. Each reflects the intimacy of family. In addition to their financial sacrifice, these women were present at his death, prepared him for burial, and visited his grave. This is what a family does. Family members stick with you and are not afraid to sacrifice. Jesus is not ashamed to call such people family. Whether in giving or receiving, he does not overlook them. He loves them. His heart is drawn to them.

Jesus looks on those who are easily overlooked. This timeless principle is good news for us. In the case of these early female disciples, Jesus's love isn't extraordinary merely because of their gender. The first-century cultural context simply isolates the principle to a particular demographic. What's impressive is Jesus's love toward people who don't have anything to commend them to God. But this wasn't limited to his earthly ministry. As Thomas Goodwin says, "His heart, in respect of pity and compassion, remains the same it was on earth."[7] His heart in heaven is the same as it was on earth. This is good news.

Consider again how Jesus sees his people. Many are overlooked by those who are consumed with this world, but to Jesus they are the apple of his eye. Not only is Jesus not ashamed of you, dear Christian disciple, but he loves you. He accepts and appreciates your service to him. He draws near to you, even when others fail to notice you. You are not unimportant in his eyes.

"Take Heart. Get Up; He's Calling You"

"And Jesus stopped" (Mark 10:49). Stopping is not something particularly noteworthy unless you rarely do it. Readers of Mark's Gospel find Jesus moving with tireless zeal. Mark makes this point with one of his favorite transitions: *immediately*, a word he uses liberally.[8] But here in Mark 10, we find Jesus stopping. What's going on?

---

7 Thomas Goodwin, *The Works of Thomas Goodwin,* 12 vols. (Edinburgh: James Nichol, 1862), 4:95.

8 Mark uses *euthus,* translated almost exclusively as *immediately* in the ESV, forty-two times (compared to twelve in the other Gospels), which creates a cadence of quickness in his account.

Jesus was on his way to Jerusalem, where he would be betrayed, delivered over to death, and crucified. He knew this. As he progressed to the capital city, he was marching to his own funeral. Certainly, he had much on his mind and heart. At this point in the narrative, he was in the town of Jericho, about fifteen miles from Jerusalem. We learn that Jesus was accompanied by his disciples and a crowd of people—a large crowd according to Mark (10:46). It was not uncommon for a teacher to engage in peripatetic instruction with his disciples, teaching them as they walked along. His hour of death was at hand, and many people surrounded him as he left Jericho.

Here we are introduced to the reason why Jesus stopped. As with the examples considered above, we're a bit surprised at what captures Jesus's attention. A man was sitting by the side of the road where Jesus was traveling. At first glance, we might not notice him, but Jesus did. He's the reason Jesus stopped in his tracks. We learn his name and his situation.

His name was Bartimaeus, and he is the only person healed by Jesus in the Synoptic Gospels to have his name included.[9] The name itself isn't significant. The Aramaic term *bar* means "son of," so *Bartimaeus* actually only tells us the name of his father: he's the son of Timaeus. But, in light of the story, it's noteworthy that no other name is given. In other words, he's *not* Simon Bartimaeus (Simon the son of Timaeus). He was simply known as the son of Timaeus. Perhaps this contributes to the underlying relevance of what's happening with Jesus: he takes notice of no-names.

9   James R. Edwards, *The Gospel according to Mark,* Pillar New Testament Commentary (Grand Rapids, MI: Eerdmans, 2002), 328.

We also learn about his situation. Bartimaeus was a poor, blind beggar sitting by the roadside asking for alms. Everything about him communicates insignificance. In a crowd, it's not hard to overlook a guy like this. We expect him to go unnoticed.

But from his seat on the side of the road, he not only heard the crowd approaching, but he also "heard that it was Jesus of Nazareth" (Mark 10:47). The name *Jesus* was common, but Jesus *of Nazareth* was known for his power to heal and his heart to help people in need. Evidently, Bartimaeus had heard stories about Jesus because he began crying out to him, "Jesus, Son of David, have mercy on me!" (10:47).

As we saw earlier in the story with the children, the crowd quickly attempted to silence him. Mark tells us, "Many rebuked him, telling him to be silent" (10:48). Someone today might say, "Shut up! What's wrong with you?" We don't know why they attempted to quiet him. Maybe they thought he was rude, a distraction, or an embarrassment. But we do know Bartimaeus wasn't having any of it. "He cried out all the more, 'Son of David, have mercy on me!'" (10:48). Their resistance only fueled his persistence. The lame man used his voice as his legs and arms to run and clasp onto Jesus from his roadside seat.

Overcoming the crowd's opposition, the cries of the seemingly invisible beggar reached the ears of Jesus. Then Mark writes, "And Jesus stopped and said, 'Call him'" (10:49). At that moment, with the cries for mercy hanging in the air, Jesus stood still. Everyone else walked past Bartimaeus, but Jesus stood still. They wanted to quiet him, but Jesus called for him. The blind beggar of Jericho stopped Jesus in his tracks. He was attentive to his cries for mercy. In his customary eloquence, Charles Spurgeon observes, "I have heard of Joshua who said, 'Sun, stand thou still upon Gibeon' . . . but I rank the blind beggar above Joshua, for he causes the Sun of righteousness to stand still."[10]

Most of us have been spoken to directly by someone begging for money. Few of us have stopped. We have our reasons, and I'm not here to scrutinize them. Instead, consider that while most people aren't quick to honor beggars, Jesus is. He's the King of the universe. He created the world and sustains all things in it (Col. 1:16–17). He deserves the highest honor, and yet his ear is attentive to the cry of a poor, begging man. None of us can claim that we are too insignificant, too unimportant, too ordinary, or too poor for Jesus. He stopped for Bartimaeus. He stops for those in need. He's not ashamed of the one who cries for mercy, whatever their station in life.

The man who was hushed and hissed was now hurried to Jesus. He stood face-to-face with Christ. The scene is meant to halt us. We too are meant to stand still as our mind's eye sketches the scene. Here we find a great contrast. Bartimaeus, a poor blind beggar, was standing before Jesus, the eternal Son of God, the King of kings and Lord of lords. How would Jesus respond? Sure, Jesus heard Bartimaeus crying his name, but the Lord was doing more than simply being well-mannered. The way Jesus received the man and talked with him shows us how he looks at people like you and me. "And Jesus said to him, 'What do you want me to do for you?'" (Mark 10:51). Notice that Jesus didn't say, "What can you do for me?" Bartimaeus couldn't do anything for Jesus. He came as a needy man, and Jesus was ready to give. Jesus also didn't

10 C. H. Spurgeon, "Jesus at a Stand," in *The Metropolitan Tabernacle Pulpit Sermons* (London: Passmore & Alabaster, 1881), 27:135.

insult him or belittle his condition. Unlike the crowd who looked down on him, Jesus built him up by honoring him. Far from being ashamed of him, Jesus publicly welcomed and dignified the man.

The same is true for you and me. We sit like Bartimaeus on the side of the road, unnoticed by the multitudes, feeling the weight of our burdens on our shoulders, hoping for relief. Then we hear of Jesus, one who has a history of displaying his power and mercy. "Maybe he can help me," we wonder even as we cry and keep our distance. But Jesus's power is equal to his compassion. He is able, and he is also willing. He hears our cries for mercy, and he calls us to himself, asking, "What do you want me to do for you?" The blind man knew exactly how to answer this question: "Rabbi, let me recover my sight" (10:51). Bartimaeus wanted to see. Therefore, Jesus immediately healed him, so that he recovered his sight and followed him (10:52).

Bartimaeus joining Jesus on the path presents quite a visual. The blind man went from beggar (an outsider) to disciple (an insider). He was welcomed in as one of Jesus's followers. But notice again the question Jesus asked him: "What do you want me to do for you?" This is the same question that Jesus asked two of his disciples in 10:36. Their answer was different than the blind man's: "Grant us to sit, one at your right hand and one at your left, in your glory" (10:37). According to Jesus, they didn't understand what they were asking. They had missed the point of what it meant to follow him. Bartimaeus, on the other hand, was a humbled man. He had no interest in personal exaltation; he just wanted mercy. Thomas Brooks says, "A humble soul is lowest when his mercies are highest."[11]

---

11 Thomas Brooks, "The Unsearchable Riches of Christ," in *The Complete Works of Thomas Brooks,* ed. Alexander Balloch Grosart, 6 vols. (Edinburgh: James Nichol, 1866), 3:11.

At the close of this scene, with the former blind beggar walking with the others, we can see things more clearly. Jesus is not ashamed of people that others overlook because he longs to show mercy. Mercy glorifies God and makes the humble glad. Can't you see Bartimeaus marching out of Jericho with his face beaming and his teary eyes full of joy? Jesus is not ashamed of such people. He loves them. This is good news for people like you and me.

Consider Jesus

In each of the above sections, we see people who were on the outside looking in. Their feelings of insignificance were reinforced by their cultural moment. How does this intersect with your experience? Do you long to be noticed but feel it impossible to measure up to the expectations of others? We'll never have enough money, success, beauty, influence, or accomplishments to turn many people's heads. It's not hard to feel insignificant. It's easy to be overlooked.

But Jesus doesn't think like this. People who blend into the crowd only seem to stand out more to him. He loves to take those of us who feel invisible and place us front and center in his family photo. It's refreshing—shocking perhaps—to consider Jesus, the one who has it all and yet notices those who don't.

4

He Is Not Ashamed of Those Who Were Far from God

"MY GOD, MY GOD, why have you forsaken me?" (Matt. 27:46). In the hour of Christ's death, two things gain remarkable clarity: first, how far he had to come to rescue his people and, second, how costly his sacrifice was. As a result, we learn his love for the church. May we never forget that it was love that motivated Jesus to pursue us (John 3:16; 15:13; Eph. 5:25–26).

Jesus, the eternal Son of God, became a man. He put on flesh because we are made of flesh (Heb. 2:14). He did this for us. Thomas Watson says, "O how did Christ abase himself in taking flesh! It was more humility in Christ to humble himself to the womb than to the cross."[1] Watson's point is this: it's natural for men to die but not for God to become a man. For Christ

---

1 Thomas Watson, *The Christian's Charter of Privileges*, in vol. 1 of *Discourses on Important and Interesting Subjects, Being the Select Works of the Rev. Thomas Watson*, 2 vols. (Edinburgh: Blackie, Fullarton, 1829), 1:128.

to become man is a step of infinite humility; he could take no greater step. But it was also infinitely costly. For people like you and me, he parted with the glory of heaven, his infinite riches, the beautiful and uninterrupted intimacy of the Trinity, and the experience of heavenly happiness. John Owen explains how this teaches us of Christ's love for us, those who were far off: "Certainly Christ had a dear esteem of them, that, rather than they should perish,—that they should not be his, and be made partakers of his glory,—he would part with all he had for their sakes."[2] Jesus became a man, fully discharged every obligation of the law of God, and drank the cup of divine wrath to save sinners like you and me. The great distance and cost underscore the great love he has for those who were far from God.

Instead of being ashamed of those who are far off, Jesus comes after them. In this chapter, we'll consider a few examples that show this glorious truth.

The Prodigal Son

The parable of the prodigal son in Luke 15:11–32 is one of the most well-known examples of Jesus's teaching. The story comes on the heels of two other parables that communicate the joy experienced when something lost has been found (a lost sheep in 15:1–7 and a lost coin in 15:8–10). Both parables model the joyful reaction in heaven when a sinner repents (15:7, 10). The story of the prodigal son illustrates how unfulfilling sin is and what the posture of true repentance looks like. The parable also shows the heart of a father welcoming his wayward son home.

2 John Owen, *The Works of John Owen,* ed. William H. Goold (Edinburgh: T&T Clark, n.d.), 2:136.

Within the larger context, it continues the theme of joyful celebration over finding the one who is far away or lost. Jesus is not ashamed of those who are far from God, for his heart is drawn to them. He delights in their rescue and recovery.

The story begins with the younger of two sons coming to his father, requesting his inheritance (15:11–12). His actions are intended to jolt us. He's not merely exhibiting poor manners. Rather, he's doing something disgraceful. In a twisted, self-indulgent way, he wishes his father were dead so he could get his money. Nevertheless, the father obliges, and the son takes off into a faraway land. He goes far from his father and squanders his inheritance through "reckless living" (15:14). The foolish son disregards his father's honor, abuses his gifts, and secures a miserable future for himself. Things get so bad that he hires himself out to tend someone's pigs, demonstrating how low he has gone. Pigs were detestable, unclean animals for the Jewish people. There he sits, hungrily craving the pigs' food, but "no one gave him anything" (15:15–16). Soon after, he comes to his senses and determines to return to his father. He decides to acknowledge his sin against him and volunteer to work as a hired servant for his father (15:17–18).

Our familiarity with the parable can absorb the shock of what happens next. In an honor and shame culture, like that of the original audience, listeners would've expected judgment. Everything up to this point made perfect sense. But when they heard what Jesus said next, their eyes would've been saucers. "But while he was still a long way off, his father saw him and felt compassion, and ran and embraced him and kissed him" (15:20). The son doesn't sneak up on his father. The father sees him while he is a long way off. This means he has been looking for him. He is longing for his lost son. He has compassion on him. But notice what else the verse says. The father *runs, embraces, and kisses* his son. John MacArthur puts his finger on the issue:

> Noblemen in that culture did not run. Running was for little boys and servants. Grown men did not run—especially men of dignity and importance. They walked magisterially, with a slow gait and deliberate steps. But Jesus says "his father . . . *ran*" (v. 20; emphasis added). He did not send a servant or a messenger ahead to intercept his son. And it was not merely that he quickened his pace. He himself ran. The text uses a word that speaks of sprinting, as if he were in an athletic competition. The father gathered up the hem of his robe and took off in a most undignified manner.[3]

Why does he run? Sure, he's excited; he misses his son. But there's more to it. The father knows his son would be walking through the gauntlet of shame and sneers as he makes his way home. He runs to meet his son "in order to be the first person to reach him so that he could deflect the abuse he knew the boy would suffer."[4]

The father grabs his son and begins kissing and hugging him. He doesn't care that his son is filthy, smells like a pigsty, and hasn't made restitution. No! He's overjoyed that his son, who was far off, has come home. He calls for a party, a feast to celebrate.

What a response! Why did Jesus tell this parable? Of course, he certainly revealed the self-righteous heart of the Pharisees and

---

3   John F. MacArthur, *The Prodigal Son* (Nashville: Thomas Nelson, 2008), 113.
4   MacArthur, *The Prodigal Son*, 115.

scribes (see Luke 15:1–2) who had no category for grace (as reflected in the elder brother in the story). But Jesus was also showing his own heart. Christ is the one who receives the far-off. We deserve the shame resulting from our sinful corruption of God's good gifts and our failure to show him due honor. But on the cross, Jesus took our guilt and dishonor. Now, when the prodigal comes home, God embraces, forgives, and welcomes him. At the feast with Christ, there is no hint of shame—just joyful celebration.

The Sinful Woman

One day a Pharisee named Simon invited Jesus to dinner at his home. His motives for extending the invitation aren't apparent, but we can tell in Luke 7:39 that he is unsympathetic to the Lord. Simon is not the focus of the story, however. Instead, the spotlight is on the interaction between Jesus and a woman identified only as "a sinner" (7:37). Here again we find Jesus's heart of grace extended to those who are far off. He's not ashamed to identify with her and receive her service.

Picture this dinner in Jesus's day. Guests would be reclining on cushions on their left sides, eating with their right hands, with their feet extending away from where the food was. An open door to the home would allow people on the street to pop in, watch, or listen. A woman showed up because she heard that Jesus was at Simon's house. She doesn't say a word in the entire narrative, yet her reputation and actions speak volumes.

> And behold, a woman of the city, who was a sinner, when she learned that he was reclining at table in the Pharisee's house, brought an alabaster flask of ointment, and standing behind

him at his feet, weeping, she began to wet his feet with her tears and wiped them with the hair of her head and kissed his feet and anointed them with the ointment. (7:37–39)

The woman's specific sins are not mentioned; however, because of her public reputation, many interpreters speculate that she was a prostitute. She entered the house but did not approach the table. Instead, she stood behind Jesus and showered his feet with her devotion. Her tears flowed down on them.

Why was she crying? Jesus said her actions reflected her love for him because her many sins had been forgiven (7:47). She also poured oil over Jesus's feet from an alabaster flask (a translucent stone used to store costly perfume). She expressed her gratitude and devotion to Jesus for how he had treated her, even when she was far from God. Her heart rang out with love because Jesus received someone like her. Grammatically, Luke layers her actions to emphasize his point: "'She was wiping, was kissing, and was anointing.' The impression is that each step took some time. One can imagine the impression it made at the meal."[5]

This whole scene made Simon uncomfortable. Squirming and evaluating this interaction, he thought to himself, "If this man were a prophet, he would have known who and what sort of woman this is who is touching him, for she is a sinner" (7:39).

Jesus, reading his mind, initiated a conversation. He asked Simon who would love more: one who is forgiven much or one who is forgiven little (7:41–42). Simon picked the obvious answer, "The one, I suppose, for whom he canceled the larger debt" (7:43).

5   Darrell L. Bock, *Luke: 1:1–9:50,* Baker Exegetical Commentary on the New Testament (Grand Rapids, MI: Baker Academic, 1994), 697.

Affirming his answer, Jesus then contrasted the woman's actions with Simon's. Simon had not provided water to clean Jesus's feet (a common courtesy), yet the woman cleaned Jesus's feet with her tears and wiped them with her hair. Simon had not given him a kiss of greeting (another common courtesy), but the woman kissed his feet ceaselessly! Finally, Simon had not anointed Jesus's head with oil (not required, but again, a common courtesy), but this woman showered his feet with expensive perfume.

The lesson is obvious: this woman acted like this because she had been forgiven much. Her loving actions were her response to the forgiveness Jesus had granted her. She had an acute awareness of her sinfulness—she was far off from God—but she also enjoyed the experience of forgiveness: "her sins, which are many, are forgiven" (7:47). Jesus associated her love for him and faith in him with her actions (7:47, 50). Her deeds did not earn forgiveness. Rather, they were an expression of her faith in and love for Christ. Like every other believer in Christ, this woman was saved by her faith apart from works (Eph. 2:8–9). Whenever anyone realizes they've been forgiven much, they respond with acts of love and devotion to Jesus.

Before we move on, sit for a minute and contemplate the weight of this scene. Someone who was far from God made the religious people uncomfortable. But, not Jesus. He was neither uncomfortable with nor ashamed of her. He's right at home with people like this. We're his family.

The Unclean and the Clean

As I write, we are experiencing a global pandemic. Cases are spiking, and government restrictions are tightening. Things have changed for all of us. Because of COVID–19, we've had to constantly think about where we've been, who we've been around, what we've touched, and what has touched us. Many have had to quarantine after contracting the virus or having close contact with someone who has. Though these changes are complicated and often frustrating additions to our lives, they do provide us with a framework to understand better the experience of the people living in Israel during Jesus's ministry. Living under the old covenant ceremonial laws meant that they too had to be aware of where they had been, who they had been around, and what they had touched. If they became unclean, they had to quarantine. For them, the status of clean and unclean was not primarily about stopping the spread of disease but about drawing near to God in worship. This concept of worship helps to put in context the many instances in which Jesus cleansed people of their uncleanness.

Defining the Terms

Before considering some of these examples, it would be helpful to define and distinguish a couple of terms. When you read through a book like Leviticus, you find words contrasted like *holy* and *common*, as well as *clean* and *unclean*. Holy and common relate to a status, while clean and unclean relate to a condition.

Common was the normal state of people and things. To be common was not negative. However, once something was set apart as holy, it couldn't become common again but was dedicated to the Lord. Its status had changed. Let me give an example. The oil used for worship in the tabernacle was holy—set apart by God for worship in his presence. Since it had undergone a change in status, it could never be used for a common purpose. Thus, you couldn't take the holy oil and use it for the lamp in your house.

To be clean or unclean, however, was a condition that could change. In fact, it changed all the time. It was nearly impossible for a person not to become unclean at some point. This means that clean and unclean are not primarily moral categories. For example, giving birth to a child was not sinful, but it made a woman unclean. Touching a dead body was not sinful, but it made someone unclean. Having a skin disease was not sinful, but it made someone unclean. The categories of clean and unclean symbolize the moral impurity that bars entrance into God's presence.

LIFE AND DEATH

These laws make a clear distinction between life and death. God is the source of life, so the closer one gets to the Lord, the closer one gets to life; and the further one goes from the Lord, the closer one gets to death. So, the innermost part of the tabernacle—the holy of holies—is the nearest a person could get to life at its fullest. The wilderness outside the camp of Israel was the place of chaos and death. To be unclean was like being under the shadow of death. Consider the skin disease of leprosy (Lev. 13:45–46). The leprous person had to wear torn clothes and let their hair hang loose as signs of mourning. Until the leprosy was gone, the leper had to live outside the camp—the place that symbolically represented death and chaos. People with skin diseases were experiencing a kind of living death. Death taints everything it touches. Uncleanness casts a shadow of death over people and things. They could not come into the presence of God until they were clean again. They had to remain far-off.

HOLINESS AND POLLUTION

Uncleanness represents the pollution of sin. Many things made someone unclean—physical imperfections, loss of blood, deformities, disease—all related to the curse of sin and the effects of the fall. Without cleansing and atonement, sin made someone unfit to be in God's presence. Laws about outward uncleanness were given to teach Israel about the inward filthiness of sin. The laws sent the message: atonement is needed for sinners to enjoy fellowship with a holy God. Once someone was cleansed, they were often required to bring an offering to God. For example, after childbirth, a woman was to bring a burnt offering to the Lord (Lev. 12:6–8). The burnt offering represented consecration to God and atonement for sin (1:3–4). Why was this offering required? After all, childbirth is a blessing, not a sin. It was required because these laws were meant to teach the people about God's holiness and sin's pollution.

This is the world Jesus stepped into. When he drew near to men and women who were unclean, he drew near to those who were far from God. The stench of death surrounded them. Let's consider a few examples.

A Leper Cleansed

One day a leper knelt before Jesus and begged to be healed (Mark 1:40). In light of what we know about the religious purity laws regulating their behavior, this was not normal. This man was unclean and was supposed to be isolated away from the community. If anyone happened to come near him, he was obligated to cry out, "Unclean, unclean" (Lev. 13:45). Yet this leprous man came near to Jesus and said, "If you will, you can make me clean"

(Mark 1:40). Although he was far from God, the man had hope. He was desperate, but he had hope because Jesus was standing before him. So the leper begged Jesus to help him.

As we've come to expect by now, Jesus's response was not what we expect. Not only was he able, but he was, in fact, willing. "Moved with pity, he stretched out his hand and touched him and said to him, 'I will; be clean.' And immediately the leprosy left him, and he was made clean" (1:41–42). Jesus was "moved with pity" by this man. He felt compassion toward him. Why? Because Jesus is uniquely aware of the bitterness and horror of sin's curse. Because Jesus hates sin and its effects. Because Jesus is drawn with love toward those who live under the lingering shadow of death. Jesus felt compassion for this unclean man because his heart is filled to the brim with love for those far from God.

His pity is not a mere feeling. It does something. It acts. Jesus did what no one else would do. He stretched out his hand and touched a leper. Jesus reached out to him rather than running from him in fear or disgust. Why did he touch the leper? Calvin observes, "By his word alone he might have healed the leper; but he applied, at the same time, the touch of his hand, to express the feeling of compassion."[6] When, do you suppose, was the last time this man was touched by anyone? As a leper, he was quarantined in his uncleanness. But he was not too far for the arm of Christ to reach, and not too unclean for the heart of Christ to love. Don't miss this: the shameful move Jesus's heart. He's not ashamed of those who are far from God. He's moved with compassion for them.

6 John Calvin, *Commentary on a Harmony of the Evangelists Matthew, Mark, and Luke*, trans. William Pringle, 3 vols. (Bellingham, WA: Logos Bible Software, 2010), 1:374.

This encounter is also astonishing in the way it broke the pattern of how this clean and unclean rubric worked. Normally, when the clean came into contact with the unclean, then clean became unclean. But not here. The clean one (Jesus) touched the unclean, and the unclean became clean! This is unprecedented. Why? The power of Jesus is never overcome by a greater force because there is no greater force. How? Jesus has the ability to remove sin and all of its manifestations. It's as if a brand new, glimmering white shirt turned a load of dark-colored laundry white and not the reverse. This is a picture of his atoning work. Jesus doesn't simply scrub the exterior, but he gets under the surface, into the places of our mess and ruin—our sinful hearts— and he cleanses them (Heb. 9:13–14). He takes people like you and me, people who are far off and unclean, and brings us home to God (1 Pet. 3:18).

A Hopelessly Unclean Woman

In another scene in Mark's Gospel, a large crowd enveloped Jesus. Among the crowd, "there was a woman who had had a discharge of blood for twelve years, and who had suffered much under many physicians, and had spent all that she had, and was no better but rather grew worse" (Mark 5:25–26).

Her situation seemed hopeless. She had exhausted all her resources on all known medical options trying to remedy her increasingly worsening condition. On top of this, she was ceremonially unclean (Lev. 15:25).

But she wasn't completely without hope. "She had heard the reports about Jesus and came up behind him in the crowd and touched his garment. For she said, 'If I touch even his garments, I will be made well'" (Mark 5:27–28). "Immediately," Mark tells us, "she was healed of her disease" (5:29). "Twelve years of shame and frustration are resolved in a momentary touch of Jesus."[7]

Jesus, perceiving what happened, requested the person who touched him to come forward. The woman emerged, with fear and trembling, and fell before Jesus to explain. Jesus replied to her with such tenderness and kindness, "Daughter, your faith has made you well; go in peace, and be healed of your disease" (5:34). Her fear was countered by Jesus's gentleness. He called her "daughter." Jesus was not ashamed of her. Not at all. He called her forward to identify with her publicly and to assert that she was welcomed as part of his family.

Can you envision this anxious woman's countenance change as she heard these tender words? The shadow of death fled as the Lord made his face shine on her and was gracious to her (see Num. 6:24–26). She transformed from someone on the far-off fringes to a face-to-face family member of Jesus.

The Woman at the Well

During another day of busy ministry, Jesus passed through Samaria, where he had a memorable encounter with a woman at a well (John 4). Careful readers of the Bible will note important events occurring at a well. Several prominent Hebrew men found their wives at wells: Isaac's servant found Rebekah (Gen. 24:13–18), Jacob found Rachel (Gen. 29:9–11), and Moses found Zipporah (Ex. 2:15–22). But at this well in Samaria,

7   James R. Edwards, *The Gospel according to Mark,* Pillar New Testament Commentary (Grand Rapids, MI: Eerdmans, 2002), 164.

no one could anticipate the type of person Jesus would add to his family.

The woman he encountered was a Samaritan. At that time, the Jews didn't associate with the Samaritans (John 4:9).[8] They were viewed as unclean. For a Jew to associate with them would be dishonoring, but to drink from their water pitcher would make them unclean. Most Jews would consider anyone unclean who associated with a Samaritan. But this is Jesus, the one who makes people clean by his association with them.

Jesus talked to the woman, asking for a drink (4:7). As shocking as this would've been, it's even more shocking to read that he offered *her a drink*. This was the only water that could satisfy her soul (4:13–14). She was eager to get her hands on this water, but Jesus didn't reveal the source yet. Instead, he began talking to her about her problem. Her issue was not primarily her ethnicity but her personal sin. Jesus called out her sexual immorality (not her status as a Samaritan).

> Jesus said to her, "Go, call your husband, and come here." The woman answered him, "I have no husband." Jesus said to her, "You are right in saying, 'I have no husband'; for you have had five husbands, and the one you now have is not your husband. What you have said is true." (4:16–18)

8   After the Assyrians defeated the Northern Kingdom in 722 BC, they deported many of the Israelites and repopulated Samaria with foreigners. As a result, many of the foreigners married the remaining Israelites and blended their religion (2 Kings 17–18). The Israelites in Jesus's time viewed the Samarians as half-breeds who had compromised by practicing religious syncretism. The Samaritans developed their own religious identity based only on the Pentateuch (first five books of the Old Testament) and worshiping on Mount Gerizim (instead of in the temple in Jerusalem).

Do you see how far from God she appeared? She was a Samaritan and also a chronic fornicator. But she was not too far for mercy.

Struck to the core, she replied to Jesus's shocking revelation of her private life in amazement, "Sir, I perceive that you are a prophet" (4:19). But Jesus didn't leave her wondering about his identity. He began to explain to her, "The hour is coming, and is now here, when the true worshipers will worship the Father in spirit and truth" (4:23)—that is, true worship of God would not be tied to a physical place but to a true manner: in spirit and truth. What was "the hour" that Jesus referred to? His death and resurrection.

Just as the Father seeks true worshipers, so also at this well in Samaria the Son was seeking. He was seeking this woman who seemed so hopelessly far from God. She would likely be voted "least likely to come to Jesus." But that's okay. Jesus had come *to her*. He offered her a drink of living water. He invited her into his true, spiritual family.

What was her answer? After hearing Jesus say that he was, in fact, the Messiah (4:26), she dropped everything and ran to town to tell everyone about Jesus. As a result of her evangelism, "Many Samaritans from that town believed in him" (4:39). This Samaritan woman was the first non-Jewish missionary in the New Testament. She reached her town for Christ. But that's not all.

> So when the Samaritans came to him, they asked him to stay with them, and he stayed there two days. And many more believed because of his word. They said to the woman, "It is no longer because of what you said that we believe, for we have heard for ourselves, and we know that this is indeed the Savior of the world." (4:40–42)

Jesus went to their unclean town and stayed for two days. Why? Because he was seeking worshipers. He was seeking people to be part of his family. The background of who they were, where they were from, or what they'd done only served to show more clearly who Jesus is and how far he's willing to go to add people to his family photo. He was not ashamed to go to Samaria.

Some Implications

The incarnation of Jesus Christ proves that he loves to retrieve those who are far from God. Nothing should keep you from him. He welcomes the prodigals, the sinners, and the unclean.

Have you grown up in the church and wandered from God? Can you identify with the prodigal's selfishness and emptiness? Consider the heart of the Savior again. He comes out to meet you, bearing your shame and welcoming you home to feast with him.

Do you feel far from God because of something you've done or something someone's done to you? Consider the tender words again to the woman whose tears of love covered his feet, "Your sins are forgiven" (Luke 7:48).

This Jesus is not ashamed to call us his children. His compassionate hand extends to people like us. His heart is big enough to love you, and his arm is long enough to reach you.

5

He Is Not Ashamed of Those
Who Have Nothing

WHEN YOU SCAN THE family photo of Jesus, you see a number of people with different stories. But do you know one thing that unites everyone? None had anything to offer God. He didn't need anything from any of them. God doesn't approach salvation like a business recruiter, looking for a person with a particular skill set who would be an asset to the company. On the contrary, God saves people *despite the fact that they have nothing to give him.*

There are a couple of reasons for this. First, God is God; he needs nothing and no one. He alone is independent, self-sufficient, and eternally happy. Everything that exists needs God, but God needs nothing (Acts 17:24–25). As A. W. Tozer says, "Need is a creature-word and cannot be spoken of the Creator."[1]

The second reason relates to the nature of grace. Salvation is by grace alone through faith alone in Christ alone. Grace, by

---

1   A. W. Tozer, *The Knowledge of the Holy* (San Francisco: HarperOne, 2009), 32.

definition, is a gift. It's not like splitting the tab at lunch, where Jesus pays for some, and you take care of the rest. Grace has nothing to do with works, "otherwise grace would no longer be grace" (Rom. 11:6). Salvation is all of grace.

This is the invitation of grace throughout the Bible. The God who has everything invites us who have nothing to come and find our all in him:

> Come, everyone who thirsts,
>   come to the waters;
> and he who has no money,
>   come, buy and eat!
> Come, buy wine and milk
>   without money and without price. (Isa. 55:1)

The thirsty may come and drink freely. The hungry may eat their fill. The poor may freely come to this banquet of grace. Jesus offers himself to people who have nothing. He alone is the food and drink of eternal life (John 6:52–58). He is the source of living water, the bread of life, and the vintner of the new wine.

Having nothing may seem like a liability. But actually, in the economy of grace, it's an asset. Having nothing qualifies you to receive everything you would ever need. Imagine that.

We tend to forget this. We can fall into the trap of clinging to what we can do or have done as a basis for spiritual pride. Although we may not have actually prayed it, certainly we've echoed to ourselves the sentiments of the Pharisee's prayer, evaluating our standing before God based on our accomplishments compared to others: "God, I thank you that I am not like other men. . . . I fast twice a week; I give tithes" (Luke 18:11–12). When we raise the flag of personal merit, we eclipse the bright rays of God's grace.

Instead, we need to remember this humbling and encouraging truth: *If you are a Christian, then God loves you in spite of the fact that you have nothing to give him.* Christ is not ashamed of the poor beggars who come to him for food, drink, and clothing. He delights in receiving us and refitting us with the garments of heaven and filling us with the best foods from his royal table. The hymn writer Augustus Toplady writes,

> Nothing in my hand I bring,
> Simply to Thy cross I cling;
> Naked, come to thee for dress,
> Helpless, look to thee for grace.[2]

It's good for us to be reminded of this truth through the striking biblical narratives. May God be pleased to lift the fog of our gospel amnesia and provide a clear view of his free grace, even to those who have nothing.

The Thief on the Cross

When we come to the scene of the cross, no matter how familiar with it we are, we should find ourselves affected by the heart of Christ. After hours of interrogation, mocking, and physical torture, Jesus is nailed to the cross by his accusers. The agony of the physical pain he experienced is exceeded only by the anguish of drinking the cup of divine wrath. The Son must take the

2 Augustus Toplady, "Rock of Ages," 1776.

undiluted, fully fermented cup of divine wrath, and he must drink it dry. Obedience and love compel him. He will obey his Father's will (Matt. 26:42). He loves his Father, and he loves his people (John 14:31; 17:25–26).

Here at the cross, we once again marvel at both the manner and the recipient of this love. The love is free and infinite. And the recipient is completely undeserving.

Jesus was crucified between two criminals (Luke 23:33). They are also called "two robbers" (Mark 15:27). They were likely more than simple thieves—probably insurrectionists or possibly even murderers involved in Barabbas's rebellion (Mark 15:7). By putting Jesus in the middle, perhaps the rulers saw him as the worst of the three, giving him the distinguishing place of dishonor. Whatever the motive, they fulfilled the prophecy that the Messiah would be "numbered with the transgressors" and make "intercession for the transgressors" (Isa. 53:12). Luke records the big-hearted Savior interceding for them: "Father, forgive them, for they know not what they do" (Luke 23:34). Even here, while he was being treated as a criminal, the heart of the sinless Son of God broke for the lost. "Father, forgive them," he cried.

In the midst of his prayerful pleading, the onlookers only increased their assault. Some began dividing up his clothes and laying claims to them with Jesus hanging naked just a few feet away (Luke 23:34). The leaders, soldiers, and the crowds joined in with a cacophony of contempt: "He saved others; let him save himself, if he is the Christ of God, his Chosen One!" (23:35). Even the criminals who were crucified on his right and left poured salt into his wounds. Mark's Gospel tells us that both criminals "reviled him" (Mark 15:32). Amid their own torturous execution and with their dying breaths, these criminals, eager for some approval from the crowd and relief from their desperate condition, heaped insults on Jesus. "The men impaled on his right and left hitched themselves up, gathered in precious air, and exhaled abuse on Jesus in deadly blasphemy."[3] What a dreadful sight.

But something happened. At some point after hurling insults at Jesus, one of the criminals had a change of heart. While one criminal continued to rail at Jesus, the other fell silent. The duet became a solo. What happened? Apparently, in the span of time that he was on the cross, the thief's eyes were opened. For the first time, he saw himself rightly. But he also saw Jesus rightly. Responding to the other criminal's hateful insults, he rebuked him and defended Jesus: "Do you not fear God, since you are under the same sentence of condemnation? And we indeed justly, for we are receiving the due reward of our deeds; but this man has done nothing wrong" (Luke 23:40–41). Suddenly, this hardened criminal feared God. He saw his sin and knew that he deserved judgment. He became wonderfully self-aware. Moreover, he saw Jesus and knew that he was different. Unlike him and his companion, Jesus wasn't guilty of anything. What a blessed conclusion! He saw his own guilt and Christ's innocence. This self-awareness together with this perception of Christ's perfection are noteworthy early buds of spiritual life. In his classic book *Holiness*, J. C. Ryle observes this about the thief's words:

He makes no attempt to justify himself, or excuse his wickedness. He speaks like a man humbled and self-abased by the

3 R. Kent Hughes, *Luke: That You May Know the Truth,* Preaching the Word (Wheaton, IL: Crossway, 1998), 384.

remembrance of past iniquities. This is what all God's children feel. They are ready to allow they are poor hell-deserving sinners.[4]

If there is any confusion about this man's spiritual pulse, consider his next words. Shifting from the man furthest away, he fixed his gaze on the man in the middle and said, "Jesus, remember me when you come into your kingdom" (Luke 23:42). This is really a remarkable request from a most unlikely source. He had come to grips with his sin, saw Jesus as the true King, and wanted to join Jesus in his kingdom. He even defended Jesus like part of his family. What a remarkable change! And to think that he didn't behold Jesus working miracles but dying on a cross. He saw the glory of Christ through his humiliation. His heart had been regenerated, and he saw Christ for who he really is. Then he pleaded for the Savior to remember him. As the hymn writer puts it, "The dying thief rejoiced to see that fountain in his day."[5]

Commenting on the turn of events, Spurgeon observes, "It was strange that Christ should find a friend dying on the cross by his side."[6] In this moment of agony with the shadow of death looming, how fitting and ironic that the dying Savior would grant life to someone who had nothing to give him. Christ made a friend by conversion. Even more than a friend, Christ had a new brother.

---

4 J. C. Ryle, *Holiness: Its Nature, Hindrances, Difficulties and Roots* (London: William Hunt and Company, 1889), 269.

5 William Cowper, "There is a Fountain Filled with Blood," 1772.

6 C. H. Spurgeon, "The Determination of Christ to Suffer for His People," in *The Metropolitan Tabernacle Pulpit Sermons* (London: Passmore & Alabaster, 1895), 41:599–600.

Christ answered this prayer of faith from the dying thief, "Truly, I say to you, today you will be with me in paradise" (22:43). This was a more favorable response than the thief could've ever expected. Instead of a simple, "Yes," Jesus gave him specificity and certainty. He began with certainty, using one of his favorite expressions: "Truly"—meaning, mark it down, take this to the bank. Then he added specificity: "today you will be with me in paradise"—not next week or even in eternity, but this very day. The man need do nothing. There was nothing he could give— he was dying. Yet, Jesus granted him pardon. You cannot earn salvation. It's a gift entirely of God. If you believe in Jesus Christ, then you are saved from your sin. And when you die, you will be received by him in eternity.

> When nail'd to the tree,
> He answer'd the pray'r
> Of one, who, like me,
> Was nigh to despair;
> He did not upbraid him
> With all he had done,
> But instantly made him
> A saint and a son.[7]

This stirring narrative of the free offer of grace should remind us again that Christ is not ashamed to receive people who have nothing. See how quickly and heartily he welcomed his new brother? Let's gather up a few more falling crumbs from this scene.

7   John Newton, *The Works of John Newton,* 6 vols. (London: Hamilton, Adams, 1824), 3:580.

Our Lack Amplifies His Sufficiency

There's no better scene to make the point: Jesus loves those who can't give him anything. This guy had nothing to give—but Jesus does. He has everything. As you consider your own standing before God, don't resist the truth of your own lack. Seeing this reality isn't a curse; it's a blessing. The thief on the cross perceived his lack and was instantly stocked to the gills. When you realize that you have nothing, don't try to cover your deficiency with the camouflage of morality or religious activity. Instead, let it be a passport to grace, whereby you, like the dying thief, find your all in Christ.

Note the Unlikeliness of This Conversion

The man was a dying criminal, mocking Christ. How was he suitable for salvation? Yet, Christ saw a prospect for the kingdom, and the dying thief was plucked from the fire. Let this inform how you think about the lost around you. Also, may it serve to remind you of the unlikeliness of your own conversion apart from such grace. Spurgeon's words are wise here:

> Carefully note that the crucified thief was our Lord's last companion on earth. What sorry company our Lord selected when he was here! He did not consort with the religious Pharisees or the philosophic Sadducees, but he was known as "the friend of publicans and sinners." How I rejoice at this! It gives me assurance that he will not refuse to associate with *me*. When the Lord Jesus made a friend of me, he certainly did not make a choice which brought him credit. Do you think he gained any honour when he made a friend of you? Has he ever gained

anything by us? No, my brethren; if Jesus had not stooped very low, he would not have come to me; and if he did not seek the most unworthy, he might not have come to you. You feel it so, and you are thankful that he came "not to call the righteous, but sinners to repentance."[8]

When we behold Christ on the cross, we might be tempted to think, like the crowds, that he had nothing. But this would be foolish. While suffering for his people, he interceded for his enemies and even saved one of them. The other thief taunted him by saying, "Save yourself and us!" (Luke 23:39). But this was never possible. The only way anyone could be saved was if Jesus, the one who had everything, died in the place of guilty sinners, people who have nothing. So look again at the cross: what do you see? I see a King who's not ashamed of those who have nothing. Nor is he ashamed to stoop low and serve them. And I see my reflection there in the face of the penitent thief—a man who owed everything but had nothing to give. And yet, by grace, Christ grants me paradise. How about you?

The Kindness of the King

Occasionally when spending time with relatives of good friends, I find it hard not to marvel at the similarities between them. Whether it's the mannerisms, voice, or facial expressions, it's fascinating to watch. In the Scriptures, sometimes we see similarities between people. In one particular case, I think the resemblance between David and Jesus is striking. While not perfect,

---

8 C. H. Spurgeon, "The Believing Thief," in *The Metropolitan Tabernacle Pulpit Sermons* (London: Passmore & Alabaster, 1889), 35:182–83.

it is instructive. In 2 Samuel 9, we see a gracious king caring for someone who has nothing.

The context is important. At this point in the story, David was the king. Saul, the previous king, and his four sons had all died. But prior to their death, David made promises to Saul (1 Sam. 24:21–22) and to his son Jonathan (20:15–17) that he would not destroy their descendants. Thus, as David was enjoying God's blessings on his kingdom and no doubt musing on God's faithfulness to him, he remembered the house of Saul and particularly Jonathan. "And David said, 'Is there still anyone left of the house of Saul, that I may show him kindness for Jonathan's sake?'" (2 Sam. 9:1). Then, being more specific, David said, "Is there not still someone of the house of Saul, that I may show the kindness of God to him?" (9:3). David's motive was love, and the prototype for this love was God's own covenant love to him. In other words, David wanted to show love to someone who did not deserve it but would greatly benefit from it.

You Shall Eat at My Table Always

After inquiring, David discovered a son of Jonathan named Mephibosheth who was crippled in his feet (2 Sam. 9:3). He was permanently injured at a young age when he was apparently dropped by his nurse (4:4). Also, he was living in Lo-Debar, secluded a fair distance away from King David in Jerusalem. He may even have been hiding in fear that the new king would seek revenge against him for Saul's sake. Mephibosheth was crippled, helpless, and seemingly hopeless.

Upon receipt of the king's invitation, Mephibosheth appeared at court and fell on his face before David. What do you suppose he was thinking at this point? He was likely afraid for his life. Unaware of any existing covenant between David and his family, he probably assumed he would be executed. But to his wonder and delight, he heard his name. "Mephibosheth," said the king. Removing any potential misconceptions about his loyalty, Mephibosheth declared himself David's servant (9:6). David's answer must've been quite the shock: "Do not fear, for I will show you kindness for the sake of your father Jonathan, and I will restore to you all the land of Saul your father, and you shall eat at my table always" (9:7).

David showed him steadfast love. "I will show you kindness." This royal decree drips with grace. Instead of wrath, he would show kindness. Specifically, because of Mephibosheth's father, David would restore all that he'd lost and treat him as part of his own family.

David gave him an inheritance. The property David restored is significant. He was basically treating Mephibosheth like royalty (9:10). Formerly in exile, now Mephibosheth had a deed to what was lost. His physical condition served to highlight David's kindness. The gracious king gave everything to a man who not only had nothing but was quite needy.

David also adopted him as a son. He granted Mephibosheth a regular seat at his table. By doing this, he brought him into his family: "So Mephibosheth ate at David's table, like one of the king's sons" (9:11). Mephibosheth would join the other sons and daughters of the king around his table—the place of honor. Imagine the scene. David's handsome sons and his beautiful daughters are seated around the table, projecting the strength and beauty of the kingdom. Then, in shuffles Mephibosheth, crippled in his feet, laboring to come to the table to take the seat reserved for him. The man who had nothing and needed everything was adopted as a son. He came to eat a feast he did not deserve. This is grace.

We Are All Mephibosheths

David certainly had his share of bad days, but this day stands out as a good one because he reflects the greater David, the Lord Jesus Christ. David's kindness to Mephibosheth reminds us of how Jesus has treated us. Christians have a remarkable amount in common with Mephibosheth.

We are children of a king who lost everything. Our first father Adam was given dominion over the entire earth. As the image of God, he was to properly reflect God's character by ruling over creation (Gen. 1:26–28; 2:15). But he forfeited his position by sinning against God, and he was banished from the garden (Gen. 3). Adam went from Eden to exile.

We lived in exile. By sinning, Adam and all of his offspring fell into this state of separation. Our lives are naturally inclined toward ourselves and away from God. And while we may yearn deep within to be home with God in paradise, we hide from him, ashamed of our sin and affected by our guilt.

Like Mephibosheth, left to ourselves, we're hopeless. We don't have any way to extricate ourselves from our condition. Hopelessness and godlessness go together (Eph. 2:12). Being crippled was not a moral label: Mephibosheth didn't become handicapped because of a specific sin he committed. However, his physical handicap reflected a spiritual condition. Just as the clean and unclean laws of Leviticus 11–15 taught Israel about the inward filthiness of sin, so too Mephibosheth's condition was an outward expression of a much larger reality. This world—and everyone in it—is deeply affected by sin's curse. Spiritually speaking, we're all descendants of a banished king, exiled, and lame. Like Mephibosheth, we're helpless and hopeless on our own.

Jesus, the King of grace, calls for us. After defeating all of our enemies on the cross (Col. 2:13–14), Jesus was raised from the dead, ascended to the right hand of God, and sent his Holy Spirit. He then calls the exiled sons and daughters of Adam home through the gospel. Because of the covenant Jesus made with his Father, the banished ones come home. The King of grace wants to show people like us the kindness of God, so he calls us out of exile to his presence. And like David with Mephibosheth, he calls us by name. He knows us and loves us.

Jesus, the King of grace, gives us an inheritance. Through the gospel, believers are given "an inheritance that is imperishable, undefiled, and unfading, kept in heaven" (1 Pet. 1:4). This inheritance is far more than what Adam lost in the garden and certainly more than what Mephibosheth got from David. Through Christ, believers are granted the forgiveness of sins and guaranteed to enjoy the restored heavens and earth, where everything that was spoiled by sin will be remade by grace (Matt. 25:34; Eph. 1:11; Col. 1:12; Rev. 21:1–3; 22:1–4). There we will dwell with God forever, basking in his glory and beholding Christ's face (1 John 3:2). And even now, we have a hope of this glory, which is Christ in us (Col. 1:27).

Jesus, the King of grace, adopts us. What grace! Through Christ, believers are adopted into the family of God. Spiritual adoption reflects natural adoption; we are given all the rights and privileges of a son. He welcomes people like us, who have nothing, to come and sit at his table. Do you see the heart of David welcoming Mephibosheth to his permanent seat? He was not ashamed of what the poor man would've lacked because he delighted to show kindness. This kindness he showed was a reflection of God's kindness to us through Jesus. He is in no way ashamed of those who have nothing because he delights in giving us everything.

The King of grace, our Lord Jesus Christ, shows kindness to his people by giving them an inheritance and adopting them into his family. What a privilege it is to come to Christ, where we will eat at his table always.

Empty Hands and Full Hearts

Examples of empty hands aren't limited to these stories. Such is the characteristic of all who come to trust in Jesus. Paul reminds the church in Corinth that from a worldly sense, they weren't all that impressive: "For consider your calling, brothers: not many of you were wise according to worldly standards, not many were powerful, not many were of noble birth" (1 Cor. 1:26). Christians aren't impressive to the world around us, and neither should we be to ourselves. The reality is this: we know we're poor and have nothing.

But we are loved. Having nothing and with no way to please God, we receive everything through Christ. Look again at the dying thief, collapsing in faith on Christ and receiving an assurance of pardon and life everlasting. Christ is delighted to fill his heart with the joy of acceptance. This is one of the reasons God sends the Holy Spirit to us. John Owen says that when God pours out his Holy Spirit on us, he does it abundantly into our hearts. In doing so, he pours out the love of God in our hearts (see Rom.

5:5). The result is that we are given a "sweet and plentiful evidence and persuasion of the love of God to us." Why?

> To give a poor sinful soul a comfortable persuasion, affecting it throughout, in all its faculties and affections, that God in Jesus Christ loves him, delights in him, is well pleased with him, hath thoughts of tenderness and kindness towards him; to give, I say, a soul an overflowing sense hereof, is an inexpressible mercy.[9]

God, through the Holy Spirit, shows us that we have nothing, but he also shows us that he loves us. Far from being ashamed of those who have nothing, God delights to make known how much he loves us and that he only has thoughts of kindness toward us.

When we scan that family photo of Jesus, we see empty hands and full hearts. What inexpressible mercy indeed!

---

9   John Owen, *The Works of John Owen,* ed. William H. Goold (Edinburgh: T&T Clark, n.d.), 2:240.

6

He Is Not Ashamed of Those Who Are Weak

"I WILL BOAST all the more gladly of my weaknesses. . . . For when I am weak, then I am strong" (2 Cor. 12:9–10). The apostle Paul penned these words while experiencing intense personal suffering. He describes it as a thorn in the flesh (12:7). The word translated "thorn" is used only here in the New Testament and refers "to something pointed, such as a stake for impaling, a medical instrument, or a thorn."[1] Suffice it to say, this was incredibly difficult for Paul. But what precisely was it? Commentators speculate that it could have been physical suffering. Or perhaps it was spiritual hostility from opponents who continued to persecute him and harass the church. Paul doesn't tell us. We are on safe ground to generally conclude that the thorn was some type of prolonged spiritual or physical trial in his life.

---

1   David E. Garland, *2 Corinthians,* New American Commentary (Nashville: Holman Reference, 1999), 519.

Perhaps the ambiguity of the thorn can enable us as followers of Jesus to identify with Paul in our own experiences of weakness, so that we can also identify with him in how he was consoled.

Throughout church history, Christians have acknowledged and even boasted in their weakness. Like Paul, they learned that weakness isn't necessarily bad, for when we are weak, then we are strong.

This is a difficult concept to wrap our minds around. It's even more challenging to get it into our hearts to affect how we think about ourselves and others. We can look in the mirror and see our weaknesses and feel ashamed. *Why would God want to love someone like me?* We may also be tempted to think that weak people aren't valuable to God. *How could someone like me be useful to God? I struggle to get through the day.* We can forget both who we are and with whom Jesus chooses to identify. In the Polaroid of grace, we find weak people and a Savior who is not ashamed of them.

Boasting in Weakness Is Boasting in God

Paul's trial revealed the immensity of his weakness, but he still boasted in it. Why?

Before concluding that believers are simply strange (we are), we need to remember that there is something profound behind Paul's glorying in his weakness. When we boast in our weakness, we are boasting in Christ's strength because his power is made visible in our frailty.

John Flavel writes, "Our weakness adds nothing to God's power, it doesn't make his power perfect, but it makes it more visible, and puts forth itself more distinctly and clearly in our weakness; as the stars which never shine so gloriously as in the darkest night."[2]

Have you ever been surprised by the beauty of the stars on a clear night? A few years ago, our family was away from the city and went for an evening walk. Looking up, we were arrested by the canopy of bright, clear lights. We stopped and stared until our necks began aching. We'd never seen the stars like that. And likewise, Christians acquainted with the darkness of their weakness gain a clearer perception of the bright stars of God's power. Boasting in weakness is glorying in God's power. Indeed, you can see how Christ would not be ashamed of those who boast in God's power.

Like Paul, our trials can become a channel for realizing the sufficiency of God's grace. As God assures the apostle, "My grace is sufficient for you, for my power is made perfect in weakness" (2 Cor. 12:9).

Our Weaknesses

We contend primarily with two areas of weakness: spiritual and physical. We don't all struggle in the same way or with the same intensity, but we all grapple with weaknesses in this fallen world. This conflict will be with us our entire lives, but we needn't feel alone, ashamed, or defeated in this endeavor. Followers of Jesus Christ find solace in his promise to be with us, unashamed of us, and the victor on our behalf. We'll consider first spiritual and then physical weakness. Then we'll think together about the massive, immovable foundation of Christ's love for the weak.

2   John Flavel, *The Whole Works of the Reverend John Flavel* (London: W. Baynes and Son, 1820), 3:349. Language updated slightly.

Spiritual Weakness

In beautiful poetic fashion, the account of creation rises to a climax with God's estimation of his work: "God saw everything that he had made, and behold, it was very good" (Gen. 1:31). We then see this good creation take shape in chapter 2. God created a wife for Adam and then stationed them in the garden to work and keep it. They enjoyed God and his creation perfectly.

But then we reach chapter 3. Like ominous weather on a sunny summer day, evil is lurking. Death photobombs God's creation. God's perfect world that showcased life and joy would soon become a canvas for death and suffering. The clouds move in.

SIN AND TEMPTATION

In Genesis 3, the serpent approached Eve and tempted her to doubt the trustworthiness of God's word: "Did God actually say . . . ?" (Gen. 3:1). Then he tempted her to doubt God's goodness: "For God knows that when you eat of it your eyes will be opened, and you will be like God, knowing good and evil" (3:5). If he could make Eve doubt God's word and God's goodness, then he would have his prey.

What is temptation? John Owen describes it this way,

A temptation, then, in general is anything that, for any reason, exerts a force or influence to seduce and draw the mind and heart of man from the obedience which God requires of him to any kind of sin. . . . In particular, it is a temptation if it causes a man to sin, gives him opportunity to do so, or causes him to neglect his duty. . . . Whatever it is, within us or without us, that hinders us from duty or provides an occasion for sin, this should be considered temptation.[3]

Temptation is anything that draws us away from the obedience God requires. The serpent tempted Eve, and she succumbed to the temptation. She appraised the tree based on her authority and wisdom, and then she ate from it. Adam did the same.

They were convicted of their sin immediately. Their eyes were opened, and they were ashamed. So they hid.

Can you relate? Like Adam and Eve, when made aware of sin, believers often retreat and hide from God. We're ashamed of our sin, and we're ashamed of our temptations. Therefore, we might easily conclude that God is ashamed of *us*.

But this isn't what we find. Instead of washing his hands of them, God pursued his weak children in love. Amid the dirge of sin's apparent triumph, we hear the anthem of hope. God would not abandon his weak people but would save them (Gen. 3:15).

If there was ever a moment when you might think that God would be frustrated with humanity and hit the reset button, surely this was it. While this is a natural conclusion, it's not the biblical one. As we considered in the introduction, Jesus's bond with his people goes back before time. God knows we are weak, and he delights to be our strength.

FEAR OF MAN

In the family photo of Jesus, a great multitude of people struggle with fear. If we're honest, our fragile faith often flickers like

3 John Owen, *Temptation: Resisted and Repulsed,* ed. Richard Rushing (Edinburgh: Banner of Truth, 2007), 10–11.

a pilot light in a furnace in danger of going out. Yet, God is pleased to use us. Look around the panorama of Christ's family photo and be surprised again by whom you see. The disciples fled in fear the night Jesus was betrayed (Matt. 26:56); Peter cowered before the inquisition of a young girl (26:69–75); Paul urged Timothy not to be timid (2 Tim. 1:6–7). Reaching back in the Old Testament, we see Gideon protesting God's call by appealing to his weakness (Judg. 6:15). And who can forget Moses? When God called him to lead his people, Moses listed his résumé of weakness and begged God, "Please send someone else" (Ex. 4:10, 13).

The weakness of these biblical characters is more precisely called the fear of man (as opposed to the fear of God). Ed Welch observes that we fear man rather than God because we "see people as 'bigger' (that is, more powerful and significant) than God, and, out of the fear that creates in us, we give other people the power and right to tell us what to feel, think, and do." He then provides several different reasons for this pattern in our lives. We fear people because they can (1) "expose and humiliate us"; (2) "reject, ridicule, or despise us"; and (3) "attack, oppress, or threaten us."[4]

We tend to fear people because of something they've done to us or because of something we think they may do to us. And we fail to trust God because we forget all he's done for us and everything he's promised to us.

Can you relate? I know I can. Sometimes it seems like I've turned Proverbs 29:25 inside out to read, "The fear of man keeps me safe, but whoever trusts in the Lord is ensnared." But this is

---

4 Edward T. Welch, *When People Are Big and God is Small* (Phillipsburg, NJ: P&R, 1997), 23.

ridiculous. We know in our minds what is right: "The fear of man lays a snare, but whoever trusts in the Lord is safe."

When you spend some transparent time with other Christians, you realize that we all struggle in this area. We all fear man and fail to trust the Lord as we should. We think we have perfect vision of what's to come while being nearsighted about the past. We forget what God's done and how faithful he's been to us. And our perceived 20/20 vision of the future is clouded by anxiety and doubt. We can't see clearly through the lenses of the fear of man.

We can become discouraged when we consider our lives in light of God's standard. If we're taking an honest assessment of ourselves, we may quickly become ashamed. *Why would God want someone like me? What do I bring to the table? How could I be of any value to him? How could I possibly contribute to the team?* This is where the purposes of God are so different than ours. Jesus doesn't look at us the way general managers of professional sports teams approach the draft. They're looking at the talent and potential of prospects who can help them taste the glory of victory. Instead, Jesus has already earned the victory, and he chooses those who will bring him glory through their weakness. His prospects are people beset with frailty. Our weakness is not an end but a means to an end. It demonstrates to us and others that what God accomplishes through us is a result of his strength and not our own. Our weakness is a pathway to adorning God's power.

WEAK APPETITE FOR GOD AND HIS WORD

"I was like a beast toward you" (Ps. 73:22). The psalmist reflects on his attitude and actions, concluding that he was like an ignorant animal before God. Why? Early in the psalm, he confesses that he struggled with God's providence. Specifically, he questioned God's wisdom when he observed that many who do not love God seem to flourish, while those who do love him suffer hardship. He even admits to feelings of bitterness and frustration (73:13–15). His heart was not warm toward God or his word; instead, it was increasingly hard. His weak appetite for God was weakening daily.

Does the psalmist's experience ring true for you? Do you see things unfolding in the world and think, "That's not quite how I'd have done it if I were God"? Has doubt and cynicism crept into your heart through the unexpected turns in your life? Do you find your spiritual appetite weak?

What does God do with people like us? Does he cast us off? Does he find some new people who will never behave like beasts? Thankfully not. He meets with us, speaks with us, and changes us through our prayers, his word, and corporate worship.

For the psalmist, everything changed when he went into the temple to worship: "I went into the sanctuary of God; then I discerned their end" (73:17). In the place of worship, God met him, and he began to see God, himself, and others rightly.

> Nevertheless, I am continually with you; you hold my right hand. You guide me with your counsel, and afterward you will receive me to glory. Whom have I in heaven but you? And there is nothing on earth that I desire besides you. My flesh and my heart may fail, but God is the strength of my heart and my portion forever. (73:23–26)

When we don't feel a strong desire for God or his word, we are tempted to sit in the shadows of doubt and discouragement. We hide in our weakness, doubting God and pitying ourselves. We have to remember that our sin does not sever our relationship with God, but it does affect that relationship. Sin clouds our vision and dulls our senses. But it's foolish to remain distant from God because the way to God is the way to happiness. Like the psalmist, when we draw near to God in the word, prayer, and public worship, he draws near to us (James 4:8). When we seek him, we find him. He's not hiding from us. He's there, like the prodigal's father, waiting to receive and welcome us in his loving embrace (Luke 15:20). He's not ashamed of us. If you feel a sense of your weakness, remind yourself that you are just the type of person God delights to strengthen. Open the Bible and read the perfect word that revives the soul, makes wise the simple, enlightens the eyes, and makes our hearts rejoice (Ps. 19:7–8).

Physical Weakness

Like Adam and Eve, we first experience spiritual weaknesses and then the physical. The latter is a result of the former. The curse from sin affects everything, and our bodies join the chorus of creation's groaning cries of weakness. But physical weakness is an opportunity for us to experience Christ's compassion and power.

AGING

Consider how Paul frames the story of Abraham and Sarah. Remember, Abraham is an example of us all; we are his offspring by faith (Gal. 3:29).

> [Abraham] did not weaken in faith when he considered his
> own body, which was as good as dead (since he was about a

hundred years old), or when he considered the barrenness of Sarah's womb. No unbelief made him waver concerning the promise of God, but he grew strong in his faith as he gave glory to God, fully convinced that God was able to do what he had promised. (Rom. 4:19–21)

He says Abraham's body "was as good as dead." This makes the point well: he didn't have much to offer God. He was weak. On top of that, his wife, Sarah, was barren.

Nevertheless, he was strong in faith. Do you see the contrast? Physically weak but spiritually strong. This truth is so easy to miss: the weaknesses of our bodies are opportunities to showcase the strength of God. Faith is powerfully displayed in and through weak people.

I've had the privilege of friendships with many older saints. These dear brothers and sisters are a source of great wisdom and encouragement. They also experience the raw feelings of regret that many of us share. As their bodies age, physical challenges increase. This makes it more difficult to do many of the things they did when they were younger. It's not uncommon to get discouraged. Increased fatigue and the perception of decreased usefulness feel like tremendous weights on their backs.

We must remember the truth that Jesus is not ashamed of any of his followers. Neither age nor perceived usefulness merits his love. If we're honest with ourselves, we realize that we all could be more useful. But, remember, if we are in Christ, none of us could be more loved than we are. The purpose of any weakness brought on by age is not to weigh us down but to serve as an opportunity to display the power and grace of Christ.

If you are discouraged by your perceived lack of usefulness to God, stand in the mirror behind Abraham and Sarah and ask yourself, "What made them useful?" They grew strong in faith even when their bodies grew progressively weaker. They were humbled by their weakness and lifted by God's love for them. Dear older saint, Jesus is not ashamed of you, even in your weakness.

SICKNESS[5]

The New Testament is full of examples of Jesus healing the sick. But why does he heal people? I want to highlight three main reasons that should encourage those who struggle with sickness or chronic illness.

First, these Gospel stories demonstrate that *Jesus has the power to heal.* Sometimes Jesus heals with a word; other times with a physical touch. In every case, he demonstrates his power. But he doesn't heal everyone. How should you process this? You can take comfort in the truth that if God has chosen not to heal you now, that he most certainly will heal you as you enter into eternity.

Second, Jesus's healing demonstrates that *a new age is dawning.* Jesus's acts of healing in the Gospels are displays of the in-breaking of the kingdom of God. Reading the book of Matthew, you see the King who has the power to usher in this new age where there will be no more pain, suffering, tears, or death. Amid the flurry of healing activity in a sample passage, we see Jesus heal a leper, a paralyzed man, and Peter's sick mother-in-law (Matt. 8:1–17). When the dawning light of the new creation filled Peter's home, those who were sick or oppressed by demons were drawn to Jesus

---

5 This section has been adapted from Erik Raymond, "Why Does Jesus Heal People?," *The Gospel Coalition*, April 7, 2021, https://www.thegospelcoalition.org/.

like moths to a flame (8:16). Matthew sees this as a fulfillment of Isaiah's promised rule of the Messiah (8:17).

Finally, his powerful healings demonstrate that *Jesus has compassion.* "When he went ashore he saw a great crowd, and he had compassion on them and healed their sick" (14:14). When Jesus heals, we see his compassionate heart on display. And his heart in heaven remains as it was while here on earth. Reading these passages is an invitation to believers to "take our hands, and lay them upon Christ's breast, and let us feel how his heart beats and his bowels yearn towards us, even now he is in glory."[6] He is not ashamed of us in our weakness; instead, he is compassionate toward us.

If you are suffering from sickness or chronic pain—perhaps like the woman who spent all of her resources and got no better but only worse (Mark 5:26)—behold Christ your Savior! The one who sympathizes with you in your weakness also has sufficient power to remove your pain and suffering. And indeed, he will! The kingdom he inaugurated is speeding toward you. In the age to come, you will realize in your body what you know in your mind: the weakness, pain, and suffering that now plague you have an expiration date.

DYING[7]

As I write this, the world continues to be affected by the COVID-19 pandemic. One area that's been uniquely altered is the care for those who are dying. The American Heart Association reports that "more people are dying during the pandemic—and not just from COVID-

---

6 Thomas Goodwin, *The Works of Thomas Goodwin* (Edinburgh: James Nichol, 1862), 4:111.

7 This section has been adapted from Erik Raymond, "They Don't Die Alone," *The Gospel Coalition*, August 31, 2020, https://www.thegospelcoalition.org/.

19."[8] Deaths have increased across the board. In many cases, due to visitation restrictions, those in the final hours of life have died alone. They and their loving families have not been afforded the customary comfort of visiting, last words, and a held hand. As I reflected on a friend's death during this time, I turned over this difficulty in my mind. I wished his family and friends could've been near him. I had hoped that I, as his pastor, could've visited. I lamented how he had to walk through the shadow of death alone.

But then I remembered. As is so often the case, the trials and difficulties in this life reveal the privileged position of those who walk with God. The truth is this: God is with his people. They are never alone. I remembered the comforting words of Psalm 116:15: "Precious in the sight of the LORD is the death of his saints." This doesn't mean that God delights in the suffering of his people but that his heart is drawn to us in our suffering. The death of the saints is not a light matter; it's costly. In one sense, Christians die as all people die; it's common to humanity because of the curse. But in another sense, we don't die in exactly the same way. Christians do not die alone. Omnipresent and steadfast love rush to their bedside. The believer never escapes the tender eyes of the Lord. The nineteenth-century English pastor, Octavius Winslow, writes,

> [T]he friendship of God transcends all friendship, even as the love of God transcends all love. God loves not only the persons but the interests and concerns of His people. There is nothing, beloved, appertaining to you that Christ does not feel an interest in. He is concerned in all your sorrows, in all your trials, in

---

8   Michael Precker, "More people are dying during the pandemic—and not just from COVID-19," *American Heart Association News*, July 10, 2020, https://www.heart.org/.

all your infirmities, in all your wants, in all your temptations.
Do not think His is a divided affection. Oh, no! Your person
precious to His heart, all that relates to you is precious—your
life is precious—your *death* is precious. Can you think of the
departure to eternity of one you love with indifference?[9]

Definitely not. When Stephen stood on the threshold of death,
he looked to the heavens and beheld Jesus, alert and attentive to
his suffering (Acts 7:56). "Christ has a throne of mercy by our
bedside and numbers our tears and our groans."[10] Christ is a
treasured friend who hurries to our bedside to support us. Like a
family member who sees a relative suffering, he draws near. Like
a spouse who has shared years and years, he comes close and sees.
Our lives are precious to him because he loves us so. He values us
and loves us completely, even to the end.

Living with a sense of one's physical weaknesses is simply self-
awareness. We find encouragement when we remember that the
Lord knows whom he's dealing with. He knows we're made of
dust and not of steel (see Ps. 103:14). Through these sufferings,
saints are reminded of God's love for them.

Weakness Has a Purpose

The proper response to a biblical understanding of our weakness
is to avoid the two extremes of either an overwhelming sense of
shame or an attitude of complacency. Neither one is helpful. How

9   Octavius Winslow, *The Precious Things of God* (Morgan, PA: Soli Deo Gloria, 1994),
    401 (emphasis in original).
10 Richard Sibbes, *The Complete Works of Richard Sibbes,* ed. Alexander Balloch Grosart,
    7 vols. (Edinburgh: James Nichol, 1862), 1:67.

can we strike the proper balance? Here are a few ways to align your heart to God's word and ways.

It Displays God's Power

Seeing our weakness is an opportunity to see the armor of God's strength. Think about some extreme examples of weakness in the face of trials in the Scriptures. What sustained Daniel when he was in the lion's den, or preserved Jonah in the belly of the whale, or supported the three Hebrew exiles in the furnace? It was the power of God. Are we surprised to see weak people grow amid such difficult circumstances? "How is a weak Christian able, not only to endure affliction but to rejoice in it? He is upheld by the arms of the Almighty."[11] This was Paul's comfort amid his thorn in the flesh (2 Cor. 12:7–10). In the same way that we can't miss the stars when we look at the night sky, so also the Scriptures train us not to miss God's power when we look at our weakness.

It Draws Us to God

Paul resolved to boast of his weakness. Why? Because it was an avenue for realizing the power of Christ. "For when I am weak, then I am strong" (2 Cor. 12:10). Weakness isn't an end itself but a means to an end. Paul rejoiced because of where his weakness brought him. If mercy is what we need and difficulty makes us cry for it, then that difficulty—though unpleasant—becomes a surprising minister. It's the vehicle that brings us closer to God. Having this perspective will flavor our difficulties with heavenly seasoning.

11 Thomas Watson, *A Divine Cordial; The Saint's Spiritual Delight; The Holy Eucharist; and Other Treatises,* The Writings of the Doctrinal Puritans and Divines of the Seventeenth Century (London: Religious Tract Society, 1846), 9.

It Cultivates Joy

Amid any trial, whether spiritual or physical, believers can be confident that their struggles are not pointless. God is always doing something in and through them for his glory and our good (Rom. 8:28). Knowing and believing this will cultivate joy in our lives (James 1:2–4). When trials weigh heavy on us, this truth can be hard to grasp—especially for those who endure suffering for long seasons or even for their entire lives. If we are convinced of his sovereignty and his love for us, time and faith can help us rejoice even when sorrowful (2 Cor. 6:10). The trials are unpleasant but not pointless. They make us better. Like polishing a dirty and tarnished piece of silver with a soft cloth, God wisely uses the trials to make us shine in his use. This is a level of wisdom beyond our ability. This surprises us because God brings life out of death, healing through wounding, and heaven out of hell. "God's grace and power are never so evident in a soul as in a time of affliction."[12]

Christ Identifies with Us in Our Weakness

When God witnessed Adam and Eve hiding, he loved them in their weakness. He clothed them and promised a Savior. Even while the natural consequences for sin unfolded, the promise of hope and restoration echoed in their ears.

Christ Clothes Himself in Our Weakness

Christ is not ashamed of weak people because he identifies with us in our weakness. We see this in the incarnation of

---

12 Thomas Boston, *The Whole Works of Thomas Boston*, ed. Samuel M'Millan, 12 vols. (Aberdeen: George and Robert King, 1849), 4:333. Language updated slightly.

Jesus when God became a man. Though truly God, he added humanity. Jesus clothed himself in the weakness of our flesh. Through the New Testament's pages, we encounter Jesus, the unique Son of God, who is eternally omnipotent and infinitely glorious, displaying shockingly common humanity. Herman Bavinck observes,

> He was hungry and thirsty, sorrowful and joyful, was moved by emotion and stirred to anger. He placed himself under the law and was obedient to it until death. He suffered, died on the cross, and was buried in a garden. He was without form or comeliness. When we looked upon him there was no beauty that we should desire him. He was despised and unworthy of esteem, a man of sorrows and acquainted with grief (Isa. 53:2–3).[13]

In summary, Bavinck says, "Nothing human was strange to Christ."[14] This brings immeasurable comfort to Christians. Not only is Jesus aware of our weakness, but he is also intimately familiar with it. By taking on flesh, Jesus took on all that characterizes our weakness, yet without sin.

Christianity is full of weak people. Christ knows we're weak, and he loves us anyway. In fact, he loves us *that* way. How about that? With Jesus, there's no pretending or games, just a genuine invitation for the weak to come to him and be made strong in his welcoming and powerful embrace.

13 Herman Bavinck, *The Wonderful Works of God* (Glenside, PA: Westminster Seminary Press, 2019), 298.
14 Bavinck, *The Wonderful Works of God*, 307.

I hear the Savior say,
"Thy strength indeed is small;
Child of weakness, watch and pray,
Find in me thine all in all."[15]

Our weakness can make us ashamed, but for Jesus, it's a magnet for his mercy.

Christ Sympathizes with Us in Our Weakness

"We do not have a high priest who is unable to sympathize with our weaknesses" (Heb. 4:15). This verse should ring in the ears of everyone who senses their weakness. Repeat these words; they are a balm to the soul.

In particular, two realities can lift our drooping chins. First, instead of being ashamed of us, Jesus can sympathize with us in our weakness. This sympathy is not a distant empathy. It's a close, intimate sense of experience. Dane Ortlund's comments are helpful here:

> "Sympathize" here is not cool and detached pity. It is a depth of felt solidarity such as is echoed in our own lives most closely only as parents to children. Indeed, it is deeper even than that. In our pain, Jesus is pained; in our suffering, he feels the suffering as his own even though it isn't—not that his invincible divinity is threatened, but in the sense that his heart is feelingly drawn into our distress.[16]

---

15 Elvina M. Hall, "Jesus Paid It All," 1865.

16 Dane Ortlund, *Gentle and Lowly: The Heart of Christ for Sinners and Sufferers* (Wheaton, IL: Crossway, 2020), 46.

We're also meant to know that, in addition to sympathizing with us, Christ has personally experienced temptations himself. Our various temptations aren't unique to us; he has shared in them also. When the Son of God became incarnate, he endured temptations like ours "in every respect" yet came through them without any sin (Heb. 4:15). He was tempted, sad, thirsty, hungry, and abandoned. He knows what you are going through, and he's not ashamed of you.

John Newton, an eighteenth-century English pastor and author of the hymn "Amazing Grace," once wrote a letter to a friend who struggled with an increased perception of his weakness. He points him to Christ and in particular to the great benefits gained by his sympathy with us:

> Though he is now exalted above all our conceptions and praises, is supremely happy in himself, and the fountain of happiness to all his redeemed; yet he is still such a one as can be touched with a feeling of our infirmities; Heb. iv, 15, 16. He has not only a divine knowledge, but an experimental perception of our afflictions.[17]

Then Newton quotes the hymn-writer Isaac Watts:

> Touched with a sympathy within,
> He knows our feeble frame;
> He knows what sore temptations mean,
> For he has felt the same.[18]

---

17 John Newton, *The Works of John Newton,* 6 vols. (London: Hamilton, Adams, 1824), 6:580.
18 Isaac Watts, "With Joy We Meditate the Grace," 1709.

When Newton wrote to his discouraged friend, he was dipping his pen into the inkwell of Hebrews 4. Recognition of personal weakness, even expressed through various temptations, is not an occasion to hide from Christ. Instead, we are to realize that our sympathetic high priest knows what it's like to be tempted. He knows what it's like to feel weak. What's more, even in his state of exaltation, he is sympathetic to us in our struggles. "If Christ should not be merciful to our infirmities, he should not have a people to serve him."[19] So rather than retreating from him in shame, we can wear out a path to the throne of grace in prayer. "Let us then with confidence draw near to the throne of grace, that we may receive mercy and find grace to help in time of need" (Heb. 4:16).

Dear fellow weak believer, do you sense your weakness? Don't doubt his care for you. He's not ashamed of us; he's sympathetic toward us. For every trial, he gives us a million mercies. "The sighs of a bruised heart carry in them some report, as of our affection to Christ, so of his care to us."[20]

Therefore, as we live, persevering in weakness and clinging to Christ, we know that one day we'll join the rest of the family in the eternal Polaroid of grace. Those who were weak will marvel at God's power, shining like glittering stars wrapped in the blanket of the night sky.

---

19 Sibbes, *Complete Works*, 1:69.
20 Sibbes, *Complete Works*, 1:72.

7

He Is Not Ashamed of Those Who Still Sin

"BUT GO, tell his disciples and Peter that he is going before you to Galilee. There you will see him, just as he told you" (Mark 16:7). This is a quote from the morning of Jesus's resurrection. Three women, ever faithful disciples of Jesus, came to his tomb. They brought spices and their loving intention to honor him by anointing his body for burial. But when they arrived, they found the large stone rolled away from the entrance and an angel sitting inside the tomb. To their surprise, the angel announced that Jesus has risen, just as he had said he would. He invited them into the tomb to investigate before deputizing them to go and tell the other disciples. But in the angel's instructions, he singled out one disciple by name—the apostle Peter.

Why did he only mention Peter? Why did he mention Peter at all?

On the night of Jesus's crucifixion, Peter denied him three times. He sinned—big time. The angel singled out Peter because the risen Christ is not ashamed of his people, even those who still sin.

To appreciate the magnitude of this truth, we need to revisit the context leading up to Peter's denial. We want to think about how Jesus handled it. Peter's denial didn't surprise him; he knew it was coming. But before we consider this, I want to caution you against standing on the sidelines. When you look at the events of Peter's life unfold, don't view it like a documentary. Instead, put yourself in his shoes and see continuity with your own story.

If you are a Christian, then you're keenly aware of the reality that you still sin. But what you probably forget is that Jesus knows this too. The truth that Jesus is not ashamed of his followers even includes the times when they sin. This must be true because no Christian has ever achieved a sinless day in his or her life. To be clear: Jesus doesn't love sin, but he does love sinners. And those who follow Jesus are characterized by hating sin, especially as we face the reality of our indwelling sin (Rom. 7:15, 17). We now live in between the time of our conversion to Christ and the time of our conformity to Christ. We are waiting for and eagerly pursuing our full sanctification (Heb. 12:14), which involves a present struggle against sin. Sometimes we see victory, for which we praise God. Regrettably, many other times, we don't. In those times of sin and failure, we feel dirty, discouraged, and distant from God. When we look at our sin, we can be tempted to believe that Jesus is through with us. We can think that he's frustrated with and ashamed of us. But while we may feel frustrated with and ashamed of ourselves, we can be sure that Jesus is not. Looking at Peter, we see the kind of person that Jesus loves to stick with.

Jesus and Peter

During the Last Supper, Jesus taught his disciples that one of them would betray him (Luke 22:21–23). He even identified Judas as the one who would do it (Matt. 26:25). But after this, Jesus warned his disciples—Peter in particular—that they would desert him:

> "Simon, Simon, behold, Satan demanded to have you, that he might sift you like wheat, but I have prayed for you that your faith may not fail. And when you have turned again, strengthen your brothers." Peter said to him, "Lord, I am ready to go with you both to prison and to death." Jesus said, "I tell you, Peter, the rooster will not crow this day, until you deny three times that you know me." (Luke 22:31–34)

See His Heart in His Warnings

This passage brings remarkable clarity to our understanding of Christ's heart for his people and our hearts toward him. Jesus's heart is predisposed toward compassionate mercy, while ours are predisposed toward a deceptive self-confidence.

First, Jesus revealed to the disciples that the devil sought their harm. He was nipping at their heels and wanted to destroy them. He said Satan desired to "sift you like wheat" (Luke 22:31). While we might not use this expression today, it basically means to shake the disciples to the core. Satan intended to use the coming trial to show that the disciples were not wheat but the chaff.[1] Perhaps Peter recalled Jesus's words when Peter later described Satan as an adversary prowling "around like a roaring lion, seeking someone to devour" (1 Pet. 5:8). It would take some time and painful experiences for Jesus's words to hit home with Peter.

We also see that Jesus prayed for Peter. Although Satan wanted to wreck all of the disciples, Jesus prayed specifically for Peter (Greek "you" is plural in Luke 22:31 but singular in 22:32). Jesus demonstrates such care and faithfulness in this passage. When no one was watching, he was praying for his disciple. He saw Peter threatened, and his heart responded with prayer for him. These are the muscles of mercy at work. Richard Sibbes writes, "God is more merciful to save those that belong to him, than Satan can be malicious to hinder any way."[2] Indeed "the prayer of a righteous person has great power as it is working" (James 5:16).

We also see the intention and effect of Jesus's prayer. Jesus said, "But I have prayed for you that your faith may not fail" (Luke 22:32). Our English word *eclipse* is derived from the Greek verb (*ekleipō*) translated here as "fail." The sense is that Peter's faith would not disappear.[3] Darrell Bock observes, "It is clear that failure here means ultimate, total failure, that is, a total renunciation of Jesus."[4] Peter would fail, but his faith would not. Though it was

---

1   David W. Pao and Eckhard J. Schnabel, "Luke," in *Commentary on the New Testament Use of the Old Testament*, ed. G. K. Beale and D. A. Carson (Grand Rapids, MI: Baker Academic, 2007), 384–85.

2   Richard Sibbes, *The Complete Works of Richard Sibbes,* ed. Alexander Balloch Grosart, 7 vols. (Edinburgh: James Nichol, 1864), 7:405.

3   I. Howard Marshall, *The Gospel of Luke: A Commentary on the Greek Text,* New International Greek Testament Commentary (Exeter, UK: Paternoster, 1978), 821.

4   Darrell L. Bock, *Luke: 9:51–24:53,* Baker Exegetical Commentary on the New Testament (Grand Rapids, MI: Baker Academic, 1996), 1742.

little, it would remain. Through his praying, the faithful high priest blew life into Peter's flickering flame of faith. The pilot light of faith, though dim, was still lit.

But Jesus also predicted that Peter would repent: "when you have turned again," referring to Peter's return *after* his denials. Jesus was not describing a future conversion—for Peter was already a believer—but a future return from his waywardness. Jesus knew what was going to happen and still didn't write him off. He's not ashamed of him. As we'll see, Christ himself would welcome this return. Mark it down: Jesus knows our worst days and still loves us. He loves us in them and through them.

Finally, we see that Jesus had work for Peter to do when he returned: "When you have turned again, strengthen your brothers." Though Peter would sin, Jesus wasn't done with him. Sin doesn't disqualify believers from usefulness in Christ's kingdom. He can use warped arrows to hit the mark. And he's not ashamed to do it.

Peter's Prideful Smokescreen

The sin of pride can cloud our vision. Peter couldn't see the threats. He didn't hear the warnings.

First, he missed the external threat from Satan. Jesus made an astounding statement (Luke 22:31) that Peter just glossed over. Even with Jesus saying Peter's name twice for emphasis, he still managed to miss it. The Lord told him that Satan was coming for them, but Peter was dismissive.

He also missed the internal threat. Jesus warned him of the dangerous tendency of his heart to betray him. But instead of truly hearing Jesus, Peter sped past the warning sign and attempted to defend himself, saying that he would even be willing to die for

Jesus (22:33). I don't doubt his sincerity, but sincerity can't make up for what weakness lacks. Peter modeled something that is common for many of us, a dangerous overconfidence in ourselves. We overestimate our ability to deliver on our promises. Walking around in a smokescreen of his own pride, Peter couldn't see four feet in front of him, never mind four hours ahead.

But Peter missed something else. He failed to see Christ's persistent, loving heart toward him. Jesus warned Peter of his extreme vulnerability. But at the same time, Jesus meant to show Peter that although he would sin, Jesus wouldn't abandon him. That's an astounding truth. But Peter missed it. Read Luke 22:31–34 again:

> "Simon, Simon, behold, Satan demanded to have you, that he might sift you like wheat, but I have prayed for you that your faith may not fail. And when you have turned again, strengthen your brothers." Peter said to him, "Lord, I am ready to go with you both to prison and to death." Jesus said, "I tell you, Peter, the rooster will not crow this day, until you deny three times that you know me."

We see Peter's danger and, at the same time, Jesus's devotion to him. Yet, Peter shook him off. It's like Peter was saying, "No, Jesus, you don't need to pray for me (maybe these other guys, but not me). You can count on me." There's a lesson here for us: the sin of pride will cause us to overestimate our devotion to Christ and underestimate Christ's faithfulness to us. We must never become so numb to the presence of pride that we fail to perceive its deteriorating influence on us.

With Peter's confident assertions of fearless devotion still lingering in the air, Jesus set the matter straight: "I tell you Peter, the rooster will not crow this day, until you deny three times that you know me" (22:34). Before the morning dawned, Peter would deny Jesus. The Lord knew this and still loved him.

Peter Denies Christ

Even more egregious than the pride of presumption was Peter's act of denial. He boasted that he'd be fearlessly devoted to Jesus—even to death. But instead, we find him cowering in fear of a servant girl.

After Jesus's arrest, the soldiers brought him into the high priest's house for interrogation. Luke tells us that Peter "was following at a distance" (Luke 22:54). Here we see a display of Peter's desire to follow Christ into great danger; however, as is often sadly the case, our wills can't keep up with our desires. In the scene that follows, Peter crumbled under pressure and denied knowing Jesus.

> Then they seized him and led him away, bringing him into the high priest's house, and Peter was following at a distance. And when they had kindled a fire in the middle of the courtyard and sat down together, Peter sat down among them. Then a servant girl, seeing him as he sat in the light and looking closely at him, said, "This man also was with him." But he denied it, saying, "Woman, I do not know him." And a little later someone else saw him and said, "You also are one of them." But Peter said, "Man, I am not." And after an interval of about an hour still another insisted, saying, "Certainly this man also was with him, for he too is a Galilean." But Peter said, "Man, I do not know

what you are talking about." And immediately, while he was still speaking, the rooster crowed. (22:54–60)

In a period of over an hour, Peter denied Jesus three times. There is a warning in this text for every follower of Christ: never presume on your own strength. Peter touted his faithfulness, but in the hour of difficulty, his flesh failed. In the midst of his denial, the word of God proved true, and the rooster crowed.

Christ Looks to Peter

Don't miss a tiny but significant detail in the next verses. Only Luke records it: "And the Lord turned and looked at Peter" (Luke 22:61).

Jesus was in Caiaphas's house, a man of sorrows approaching his death. At the precise moment of Peter's denial, the rooster crowed, and Jesus, likely looking out the window, locked eyes with the apostle.

How do you think Jesus looked at Peter? Was Jesus surprised? Frustrated? Ashamed? If you are a Christian, then your understanding of how Jesus looked at Peter is foundational to your perception of how he looks at you when you sin.

While we can't know with certainty how Jesus looked at Peter, I think we can make a reasonable deduction based on who Jesus is, how Peter responded, and how Jesus pursued him after his resurrection. I agree with Charles Spurgeon, who says, "I think it was a heart-piercing look and a heart-healing look all in one,— a look which revealed to Peter the blackness of his sin, and also the tenderness of his Master's heart towards him."[5]

---

5 C. H. Spurgeon, "Peter's Fall and Restoration," in *The Metropolitan Tabernacle Pulpit Sermons* (London: Passmore & Alabaster, 1902), 48:138.

THIS LOOK WAS HEART-PIERCING

God's law reveals sin. It shines a light on our actions and exposes them for what they are. It shows our sin to be exceedingly sinful (Rom. 7:13). When we peer into the word of God, we see who God is: his character is revealed to us. At the same time, we see who we are: we see ourselves in light of God's character. This simultaneous beholding of God and ourselves is unnerving. It made Adam and Eve want to hide in the garden. It made Isaiah cry out, "Woe is me! For I am lost; for I am a man of unclean lips, and I dwell in the midst of a people of unclean lips; for my eyes have seen the King, the LORD of hosts!" (Isa. 6:5). Looking at ourselves in light of God's law, we experience the unsettling sense that someone is staring at us. We perceive the omnipresent eyes of holiness locked on us.

When Peter's eyes met Christ's, there's little doubt that he acutely sensed his sin. This is because Jesus Christ is the supreme revelation of God (John 1:18; Heb. 1:1–3). He perfectly reflects and represents God (John 14:9; Col. 1:15). When Peter saw Jesus, he saw God incarnate, the Word made flesh (John 1:14), the one whom the law aimed to reveal. This is why John Newton writes of Peter, "When the servants spoke to him, he cursed and swore; but when Jesus looked upon him, he wept."[6] As Spurgeon said, the look was heart-piercing.

THIS LOOK WAS HEART-HEALING

In addition to this look being heart-piercing, it was also heart-healing. Too often, even as Christians, we think of God only as a

---

6 John Newton, *The Works of John Newton,* 6 vols. (London: Hamilton, Adams, 1824), 2:577.

judge. But what do we learn from the Scriptures? The God who is righteous is also loving. He never loves at the expense of his holiness, but his love is perfectly holy. What happened in the garden when our first parents sinned? God pursued them in love, preached the promise of the gospel to them, and clothed them with new garments of another (Gen. 3:8–21). This is the promise and picture of salvation. Or consider what happened to Isaiah when he saw the Lord in his glory and himself in his sinfulness. The angel fetched coal from the altar and touched Isaiah's mouth with it, removing his guilt and atoning for his sin (Isa. 6:6–7).

The same loving Lord confronted Peter. As the eyes of Christ our Lord met Peter's, I believe he looked on Peter with loving compassion. The omnibenevolent one beheld Peter, and his face said,

> And yet I love thee, Peter, I love thee still! Thou hast denied me, but I look upon thee still as mine. I cannot give thee up. I have loved thee with an everlasting love, and, notwithstanding all thine ill-conduct towards me, I am looking for thee, and expecting to receive thee. I have not turned my back on thee.[7]

Despite Peter's sin, Christ would not abandon him. In Peter's darkest hour, the eyes of mercy peered out Caiaphas's window and locked on him. For Peter, and every other Christian, all of God's acts are mediated through his love. His love was meant to pierce and heal the apostle.

As you think about your own life, can you relate to Peter? Perhaps your sin has not been as public and pronounced as Peter's.

7 C. H. Spurgeon, "Peter's Restoration," in *The Metropolitan Tabernacle Pulpit Sermons* (London: Passmore & Alabaster, 1888), 34:404.

Nevertheless, see that Christ's heart is equally as inclined toward you. He wants to convince you of both the seriousness of your sin and the steadfastness of his love.

The Forgiveness of Christ

Remember how we began this chapter? "But go, tell his disciples and Peter that he is going before you to Galilee. There you will see him, just as he told you" (Mark 16:7). The angel sent the disciples to Galilee to meet their resurrected Lord. The final chapter of John's Gospel opens with several of the disciples in Galilee, presumably, waiting on their Lord. As they waited, they went fishing in a boat and caught nothing after a long night. Early in the morning, a voice from the shore called, asking about their success and offering them advice. Listening to this man's instructions, the disciples cast their net and caught over 150 fish! This surprising development brought the stranger on the shore into sharp focus. John said, "It is the Lord!" (John 21:7). When Peter heard this, he jumped into the water and swam the hundred yards to the shore to meet Jesus. What would make a man like Peter act like this? He was a rugged and burly fisherman.[8] Yet he couldn't wait to get to Jesus.

After preparing and serving breakfast to his disciples, Jesus turned to Peter and asked him some questions, teaching him about forgiveness and restoration. This was not only an important time in Peter's life but also for the other disciples. Just as Peter (before denying Christ) boasted in front of the disciples of his faithfulness

---

8   In addition to jumping in the water and swimming to the shore, Peter hopped in the boat and hauled the net ashore. John includes the detail that this net was "full of large fish, 153 of them" (John 21:11).

to Christ, so too Jesus restored him publicly.[9] Jesus wanted Peter and the disciples to know that he forgave him. This is the type of love that Jesus has for his people. He wants the sinner *and his brothers and sisters* to know that he's not ashamed of them. He welcomes his repentant children home.

Jesus asked Peter, "Do you love me more than these?" (John 21:15). It seems best to take Jesus's question as, "Do you love me more than these disciples do?" rather than, "Do you love me more than you love these disciples?" or "Do you love me more than these (the fishing gear or profession)?" You'll recall that Peter boasted of his superior allegiance, and by implication his superior love, compared to that of the disciples (Luke 22:33). With the events of the last week, Jesus asked Peter, "Do you still boast in your superior love for me?"

Peter's answer doesn't reveal a hint of his characteristic self-confidence. Instead, it shows a refreshing self-awareness. He'd tasted the concrete after falling on his face. He'd been humbled. Instead of boasting in what he had done or even hoped to do for Christ, he simply said, "Yes, Lord; you know that I love you" (John 21:15). He appealed to Christ's knowledge of his imperfect yet present love. He said in effect, "Lord, you know me better than I know myself. You know that I love you, however weak and flawed. Nevertheless, it is true: I do love you, Lord."

Jesus questions him twice more, along the same lines. Each time, Peter answered in the affirmative, "Yes, Lord; you know that I love you" and "Lord, you know everything; you know that I love you" (John 21:16, 17). Why did he repeat the question three

---

9   D. A. Carson, *The Gospel according to John,* Pillar New Testament Commentary (Grand Rapids, MI: Eerdmans, 1991), 675.

times? Because Peter denied him three times (Luke 22:54–60). The same heart-piercing eyes of Christ were now continuing to heal his heart. Before the watching eyes of the disciples and the contrite apostle Peter, the great physician was dressing the wounds of sin. The one who healed physical wounds with a word was now healing the spiritual cuts from sin's sword.

Jesus not only questioned Peter about his love, but he also gave him work to do. We see three questions about his love, three professions of love, and three assignments. Jesus told Peter, "Feed my lambs," "Tend my sheep," and "Feed my sheep" (John 21:15–17). The image is clear: Peter was to be a shepherd of the flock of God. He was to take care of the precious sheep of the good shepherd. Jesus transformed Peter "from a fisherman to a shepherd, for fish die when they are caught. The sheep must be fed and cared for."[10] And notice how intimate the assignment is. "The sheep are Christ's sheep, not Peter's. Not, Tend your flock, but Tend my sheep."[11]

You and I might be tempted to believe that our sin not only bars us from the experience of Christ's love but also from usefulness in his service. But this is not the case. It can't be. The story of the apostle Peter teaches us that there is far more grace in Jesus than there is sin in us. He knew what Peter would do, and yet he still loved him through it. The Lord predicted not only Peter's sin but also his return and his usefulness to him. Remember: Jesus told Peter that after he returned, he would need to strengthen his brothers (Luke 22:32). And this is exactly what we find here.

There's no better way to keep you from the joy of knowing Christ than to tie the weight of guilt to your back. You'll never

10   C. K. Barrett, *Essays on John* (London: SPCK, 1982), 165.
11   Barrett, *Essays on John*, 166.

get above the water. You'll sink in despair and feel guilty for doing so. If the enemy can convince you that you are hopeless in your sin, then he can deprive you of one of the great privileges of following Jesus. Look again at the apostle Peter, sitting in the sand with Jesus, humbled and healed by such unspeakable love. This is your Savior, dear Christian. When you see that he's not ashamed of you, even when you sin, you'll melt in loving gratitude and be fueled for zealous service.

Jesus and His Church

Church discipline. When you read these words, what comes to mind? Probably something negative. But what if church discipline wasn't intended as a negative at all but something positive?

The process of church discipline is summarized in Matthew 18:15–20. When a church member sins, another church member is to bring the matter to his attention, privately, appealing to him to repent of his sin. If the sinning brother repents, then that's that (18:15). But if he persists in sin, the fellow church member should take one or two others from the church to likewise encourage repentance (18:16). If he still refuses to listen to this small group, then the matter is brought to the church, where they will again urge their fellow member to repent. Finally, if the person will not listen to the rest of the congregation, he is to be removed from the church because he is demonstrating a failure to submit to the lordship of Christ in his life (18:17–20).

In what way is this positive? I believe that Jesus instituted church discipline both to maintain the holiness of the church and to remind his people that he forgives them as they repent of their sins and submit to his lordship. We often focus on the first aspect—admonishment over sin that could end in excommunication. While this should get our attention and produce holy sobriety within us, it's not the whole story. At each step, the goal is clearly restoration. The burden of the faithful church members in the process is to persuade their sinning brother to forsake sin and submit to Jesus. Just as excommunication pivots on the truth that Christ is holy, so too restoration hinges on the truth that he is forgiving. He delights to forgive his people of their sins.

To see this emphasis, consider the literary context of Matthew 18. In the verses just before Jesus's instruction on discipline, he taught that the Father is like a shepherd who pursues the sheep that wander away (18:12). Then in the passage immediately following, Peter asked how many times they need to forgive people when they sin. Surprisingly, Jesus told Peter that he should forgive those who sin against him not simply "seven times, but seventy-seven times" (18:22). In other words, you don't keep count. Because God has forgiven you such a great debt, you must forgive others. Jesus punctuated this with a parable about someone who was forgiven a great amount but then was merciless to one who owed him a debt (18:23–35). The lesson is clear: forgiven people forgive. When you look at the overall context, we see that church discipline is less like a criminal prosecution and more like a rescue mission. Throughout the process is the reminder that God forgives sinners—even after they are converted. If we reflect Christ's heart, then we gently and lovingly pursue our wayward brothers and sisters, urging them to submit to his word and receive his restoration (Gal. 6:1). Jesus isn't ashamed of those who still sin. He's the one who pursues the wandering sheep. He forgives the sinner "seventy-seven times." He removes the debt of "ten thousand talents" (Matt. 18:24).[12] When you think about church discipline, see Christ's desire for a holy people. But at the same time, don't miss his heart to forgive sinners.

Conclusion

Run your finger across the pages of the Bible, and you find many examples to prove that God delights to lavish his forgiveness on sinners. Even after they commit to following God, many believers fall on their face, only to be lifted up again by the staggering love of God. Adam sinned in the garden, yet God pursued him and preached the promise of the gospel to him (Gen. 3:1–15). Abraham lied about his relationship to Sarah—twice! (Gen. 12:11–19; 20:1–12). Moses disobeyed God and struck the rock (Num. 20:8–12). David committed adultery and murder (2 Sam. 11:1–27). Jonah disobeyed God's call (Jonah 1:1–3). Thomas doubted, even when standing before the risen Lord (John 20:24–25). All of these examples remind us that though our sins are heinous, they can never separate a true believer from God. He delights in pardoning us in Christ.

With so many examples and such clarity in the Bible, why do we so often remain discouraged? Is it because you think that you will not only lose fellowship with God but lose God himself? Friend, your sins didn't prevent God from loving you before, and they won't prevent him from loving you now. Sins shall never sever God from his people. "Their sins may cause a strangeness between God and them, but shall never cause an enmity; their sins may hide God's face from them, but shall never turn God's

---

12 A talent was equal to about twenty years' wages. Ten thousand talents is intended to be an incalculable sum.

back upon them: those whom God loves, he loves unto the end: 'I am the Lord that changeth not,' saith he."[13]

Dear friend, are you living beneath your privileges in Christ? Are you stuck with your head down in the mire of guilt and shame? Look up and lock eyes with Christ through his word. Like Peter, let your heart be both pierced and healed by him. Peter denied Christ that night, but Christ didn't deny Peter. He's not ashamed to have you. "The saying is trustworthy and deserving of full acceptance, that Christ Jesus came into the world to save sinners" (1 Tim. 1:15).

---

13 William Bridge, *A Lifting Up for The Downcast*, Vintage Puritan (Louisville: GLH, 2014), 53.

8

Whom Is Jesus Ashamed Of?

IS JESUS ASHAMED OF ANYONE? After reflecting on many different stories demonstrating Christ's staggering love, we might conclude that no one will escape his loving acceptance.

But this is false.

Jesus spoke to this issue clearly: "For whoever is ashamed of me and of my words, of him will the Son of Man be ashamed when he comes in his glory and the glory of the Father and of the holy angels" (Luke 9:26).

Whom does Jesus say he'll be ashamed of? *Those who are ashamed of him.* The context around this verse sheds light on what it means. In the previous verses, Jesus explained his requirements for those who would follow him: "If anyone would come after me, let him deny himself and take up his cross daily and follow me" (9:23).

Jesus is simultaneously broad and narrow in his invitation. His invitation is inclusive: "If *anyone* would come after me." None are excluded. It's wide open. But then things tighten. There's a wide *who* but a narrow *how*. Jesus lays out three particular conditions for discipleship: *deny yourself, take up your cross (daily),* and *follow me.*

To *deny yourself* requires you to relinquish self-authority and self-ambition. It means repudiating ourselves as the center of our universe and, instead, putting Christ in his proper place. Self-denial is more than depriving ourselves of certain things. It's about orientating our entire lives around Christ.

First-century hearers would've clearly understood the words *take up your cross.* Under Roman rule, crosses were ubiquitous in the landscape. They communicated the authority of Caesar and the shame and weakness of those who died on them. When Jesus said you must take up your cross, he meant that any would-be follower must be willing to suffer the shame—even to the point of death—of following him. Jesus is looking for disciples who see him and say, "He's worth it. I'd rather die than be unfaithful to him."

Finally, Jesus said that a disciple must *follow* him. This means to line up behind him and continue with him. To follow Jesus is to receive him and his words. We must be convinced of his worth, the truthfulness of his words, and the sufficiency of his work. This translates into devotion, endurance, and faithfulness.

When Jesus said, "whoever is ashamed of me and my words" (Luke 9:26), he was referring to those who reject him. This is the opposite of following him. Refusing to follow Jesus is rejecting him. We might prefer a middle ground between following and rejecting, but Jesus doesn't allow any. Either you follow him, or you repudiate him. There's no gray area, no ambiguity. You're either with him or against him. We can see this in the words that follow: "For whoever would save his life will lose it, but whoever loses his life for my sake will save it. For what does it profit a man if he gains the whole world and loses or forfeits himself?" (9:24–25). The fulcrum for these verses is what people do with Jesus. One may save his life (i.e., choose not to follow Jesus to avoid suffering), but in the end he will lose his life because he won't have Christ. On the other hand, the one who loses his life *for the sake of Christ* saves his life. One's soul is infinitely more valuable than any earthly treasures. And the only way anyone can have eternal blessing is through Christ.

Whom is Jesus ashamed of? He's ashamed of those who reject him. According to Jesus, the people who are ashamed of him are those who refuse to deny themselves, take up their cross, and follow him. They've considered Jesus unworthy of their devotion and obedience. They reject Christ and refuse to follow him by faith. On the day of judgment, Jesus will be ashamed of those who are ashamed of him in this life.

I can't think of a more unsettling scene than standing before the Lord Jesus Christ on judgment day and hearing him say, "I never knew you; depart from me" (Matt. 7:23). Imagine Jesus the judge saying, "You were ashamed of me and my words in your life, and now, throughout all eternity, I am ashamed of you."

These words should make us pause. We should reflect on our lives. Do we genuinely believe the gospel? Do we trust and treasure Jesus?

When someone is ashamed of Christ, what does it look like? What are the symptoms? Do we have any examples? To help us with this personal diagnostic, we'll consider some of the signs and examples of being ashamed of Christ. We'll look at three main areas: being ashamed of his *worth*, *authority*, and *heart*.

Those Who Are Ashamed of Christ's Worth

Christ's worth corresponds with his glory. When we talk about God's glory, we're referring to his beauty, weightiness, and value. We testify to God's glory when we marvel at the mountains, ocean, or even a sunset (see Ps. 19:1–6). When we stare at these wonders, we are taking in God's creative glory. At various times in the Bible, we see the glory of God shine forth in other ways. When God gave the law to Moses, his glory descended on Mount Sinai (Ex. 24:12–18). At the dedication of the temple, God's glory so filled the place that the priests could not even stand to minister (1 Kings 8:10–11). Why? Because of the overwhelming sense of God's transcendent holiness. When God reveals his glory—whether in the irrepressible power of a thunderstorm or the filling of the temple—the response is always the same. People are shaken. It gets their attention. His glory reveals his infinite power and value, as well as our finiteness and vulnerability.

God's ultimate revelation of his glory may be surprising. He chose to manifest his glory supremely in Jesus of Nazareth. The apostle John writes that when Jesus came into the world, he displayed the glory of God: "And the Word became flesh and dwelt among us, and we have seen his glory, glory as of the only Son from the Father, full of grace and truth" (John 1:14). Being "very God of very God," as the Nicene Creed says, the Son became flesh. God became a man. And in this way, Jesus revealed the glory of God. Jesus perfectly displayed the beauty, weightiness, and value of God.

There were some arresting displays of his glory, like at Jesus's birth (Luke 2:9), at his transfiguration (Matt. 17:1–8), after his resurrection (Luke 24:30–51), and at his ascension (Acts 1:9; 1 Tim. 3:16). However, much of what we see from Jesus in the Gospels is a man who showed us the glory of God's heart. He displayed God's glory as he taught the Scriptures, obeyed them perfectly, loved others, and healed those who were afflicted. On the night before his death, Jesus wrestled with the infinite value of God's glory and the infinite pain of drinking the cup of judgment for sinners (Matt. 26:39). Looking back at his life, Jesus said that he glorified his Father—even as he looked ahead and prayed that God would be pleased to glorify him in his death, resurrection, and exaltation (John 17:1–5). In his life, Jesus showed God's infinite weightiness and worth. Jesus wanted those looking at the upcoming events to see his beauty, substance, and value.

If someone is ashamed of Christ's worth, he rejects his value. He doesn't see Christ's beauty. An appraisal takes place. Looking on Christ and his claims, the appraiser asks, "Is he worthy? Does he deserve first place for me?" When he answers "no" to this, he is rejecting Christ's worth.

Judas Iscariot

One of Jesus's twelve apostles, Judas traveled with him for three years before betraying him. Can you imagine how many mighty miracles and acts of compassion he observed? He saw Jesus walk on water, calm a storm, raise the dead, and weep over his friend Lazarus's death. He would've watched Jesus go away to pray all night with his Father. He had a front-row seat at countless sermons. Nevertheless, in the end, he judged Jesus to be lacking in worth. He betrayed the Son of God for the paltry sum of thirty pieces of silver (Matt. 26:14–16).[1]

Why did Judas do it? Many have speculated reasons why. It could've been his love of money, jealousy of other disciples, or frustrations over the trajectory of Christ's ministry. We don't know. But we do know this: Judas was never convinced of the glory of Christ. The man did not see the value in denying himself, taking up the cross, and following Christ (Luke 9:23). In the end, Judas was ashamed of him. For Judas—and sadly many others—Jesus isn't impressive enough. He's not worth it. What about you? Is Jesus worthy of first place? Or are you ashamed of him?

The Rich Young Ruler

One day a man ran up to Jesus, knelt before him, and asked him an important question, "Good Teacher, what must I do to inherit eternal life?" (Luke 18:18). We call this man "the rich young ruler" because the Gospel accounts together provide us with these details about him (see Matt 19:20; Luke 18:18, 23). He came to Jesus because he needed an urgent answer to this vital question.

Jesus replied by reviewing the ten commandments with him. After he recited commandments five through nine, the man confidently asserted, "All these I have kept from my youth" (Luke 18:21). But Jesus had more commandments that he purposefully held back. Jesus replied to him, "One thing you still lack. Sell

---

1   "Equivalent to about four months' wages for a laborer (about $7,500 in modern terms), this meager sum suggests the low esteem in which Jesus was held by both Judas and the chief priests." Michael J. Wilkins, study notes for the Gospel of Matthew in *ESV Study Bible* (Wheaton, IL: Crossway, 2008), 1880.

all that you have and distribute to the poor, and you will have treasure in heaven; and come, follow me" (18:22). The young man was confident in his external obedience, but Jesus pressed on his heart, showing the man his idolatry. He was covetous; money was his god. This broke the first, second, and tenth commandments. Jesus's remedy for him was to repent of his idolatry and follow Christ.[2] In other words, Jesus was telling him to turn from the emptiness of the god of money and see the worth of following him.

The man appraised the situation and declined. Putting his money on one side of the scale and Christ on the other, he weighed the matter out and found Christ lacking. When faced with the challenge and opportunity to give Christ first place, the rich young ruler declined. He rejected the chance. He did not see Jesus and treasure in heaven as more valuable than his treasure on earth.

What about you? Is there anything or anyone on earth that competes with Christ? Do you value anything so much that it makes you ashamed of Christ?

Paul's Instruction

When Paul became a Christian, he understood that his job was to testify to the surpassing glory of Christ (Acts 20:24). He did this by preaching the gospel. But he also did it by suffering (9:16). His suffering was itself a sermon declaring that Jesus is infinitely more

---

2 The Lord's instruction to the rich young ruler to sell all that he had is not a requirement for all people in order to become a disciple (see Acts 5:4). In this man's case his money was his idol; therefore, he needed to forsake it. Others have different idols that require repentance.

valuable than anything or anyone in this world. Paul showed this even at the expense of his comfort (20:22–27).

In his letters to his younger disciple Timothy, Paul urges him not to be ashamed of the Lord. How could Timothy do this? By sharing in suffering for the gospel. Paul helps Timothy see that by faithfully suffering for the name of Christ and his mission, he would demonstrate that he was not ashamed of the Lord (2 Tim. 1:8–12). On the contrary, he would show Christ as infinitely glorious!

Encouraging Timothy to see the worthiness of Christ, Paul points out several individuals who either were or were not willing to take up their cross and follow Christ. On the positive side, Paul points to Onesiphorus as a shining example of one who was not ashamed of the suffering apostle—and by implication Paul's Lord:

> May the Lord grant mercy to the household of Onesiphorus, for he often refreshed me and was not ashamed of my chains, but when he arrived in Rome he searched for me earnestly and found me—may the Lord grant him to find mercy from the Lord on that day!—and you well know all the service he rendered at Ephesus. (2 Tim. 1:16–18)

On the negative side, Paul points to several who proved to be ashamed of Christ. This would've been sobering for Timothy because he likely knew these people or at least knew of them. He mentions Phygelus and Hermogenes, who, along with many others in Asia, turned away from him (1:15). He also refers to Demas. This was a man who previously served with Paul in ministry (Col. 4:14; Philem. 24) but now had abandoned him. Paul writes, "Demas, in love with this present world, has deserted me and gone to Thessalonica" (2 Tim. 4:9). Paul reminds Timothy that "the Lord knows those who are his" (2:19).

Amid the discouragement of apostasy and unfaithfulness, Paul appeals to Timothy to "share in suffering as a good soldier of Christ Jesus" (2:3). He was to remain faithful. Then Paul says,

The saying is trustworthy, for:

> If we have died with him, we will also live with him;
> if we endure, we will also reign with him;
> if we deny him, he also will deny us;
> if we are faithless, he remains faithful—

for he cannot deny himself. (2:11–13)

Paul exhorts Timothy to remain faithful to Christ by reminding him that those who endure to the end are those who don't deny Christ. Those who deny him are the ones who don't have faith and turn away from him. This is someone who (like Judas) professes to follow Christ but finally turns away from him, or someone who (like the rich young ruler) judges Christ to be unworthy of first place in his life. Therefore, says Paul, endure in Christ. Suffer for him. He's worth it. We will reign with him. Never be ashamed of him.

Is Jesus Christ worth dying for? What about living for?

Those Who Are Ashamed of Christ's Authority

When he began his earthly ministry in Galilee, Jesus said, "The time is fulfilled, and the kingdom is at hand; repent and believe in the gospel" (Mark 1:15). Jesus was not offering advice. He spoke as a King, declaring and commanding.

We're ashamed of Christ's authority when we reject him. If Jesus tells us what to do and we disobey it, then we repudiate his authority in favor of our own. Like the appraisal of glory, the assessment of authority measures the weight of the one making the command. Rejecting Christ's lordship is rejecting his right to rule over us.

When you scan over the family picture of Jesus, you'll find imperfect people. You'll find people who rebelled and sinned against God. But you'll find people who, in the end, submitted to God's word in their lives. They valued his lordship and embraced his authority over them. Conversely, the portal into damnation will reveal this common trait for all who are there: they rejected Christ's authority. To reject his authority is to be ashamed of him ruling over you. These are the ones of whom Jesus speaks when he says, "For whoever is ashamed of me and of my words, of him will the Son of Man be ashamed when he comes in his glory and the glory of the Father and of the holy angels" (Luke 9:26).

Pontius Pilate

Pontius Pilate was appointed by the Roman emperor Tiberius to be the governor of Judea (AD 26–36). He was in Jerusalem attempting to keep the peace on the night of Jesus's arrest. The religious leaders led Jesus to Pilate, making their case for his execution (John 18:28). During his examination of Jesus, Pilate asked him about his kingdom. He was certainly concerned about potential threats to peace, but he also appeared curious about what kind of person could have the religious leaders so upset. In the end, Pilate rejected Christ's authority for his own authority (19:10). He used

Jesus as a token for political leverage to win the weekend news cycle in Jerusalem. He ordered Jesus to be flogged and attempted to wash his hands of involvement in Christ's death (19:6).

Pilate looks like many today who try to stand in a position of neutrality regarding Jesus. But such people can't get off that easy. Christ is the King of kings and Lord of lords. He has authority because he is our Creator (Col. 1:16) and Lord (Phil. 2:10–11). There's no middle ground. We either receive Christ as Lord, or we reject him. And what we do with him makes all the difference on the last day.

Professors but Not Possessors

"I never knew you." This is how Jesus wraps up his famous Sermon on the Mount. He previews the day of judgment for all those who claim to follow him but in reality don't. It's not enough to simply profess to know Christ; there must be, according to Jesus, a genuine relationship. On the last day, Jesus will not claim those who did not truly claim him during their lives.

> Not everyone who says to me, "Lord, Lord," will enter the kingdom of heaven, but the one who does the will of my Father who is in heaven. On that day many will say to me, "Lord, Lord, did we not prophesy in your name, and cast out demons in your name, and do many mighty works in your name?" And then will I declare to them, "I never knew you; depart from me, you workers of lawlessness." (Matt. 7:21–23)

What is the basis for this surprising rejection? Jesus never knew them. They are workers of lawlessness—that is, they didn't obey his word. Jesus will reject those who reject his authority. This is similar to what John writes, "Whoever says 'I know him' but does not keep his commandments is a liar, and the truth is not in him" (1 John 2:4). This doesn't mean that Jesus only receives those who are sinless (see chapter 7), but it does mean that he only accepts those who submit to his lordship (Luke 6:46). Submission to Christ's lordship looks like regular repentance from sin and a pursuit of holiness. John helpfully expounds this further,

> No one born of God makes a practice of sinning, for God's seed abides in him; and he cannot keep on sinning, because he has been born of God. By this it is evident who are the children of God, and who are the children of the devil: whoever does not practice righteousness is not of God, nor is the one who does not love his brother. (1 John 3:9–10)

If a person's life does not reflect a pattern of obedience to Christ's commands, then that person would have reason to question whether or not he is submitting to Christ's authority. Does your life reflect a pattern of submission to Christ's word? If the answer is "no," then you should be concerned about the day of judgment when Jesus will declare his assessment of your relationship with him.

Those Who Are Ashamed of Christ's Heart

As we've seen, the ministry of Jesus was compelled by love. The Father sent his Son because of love (John 3:16), and Jesus laid down his life because of love (15:13). This river of love flows into reservoirs of mercy, grace, and compassion for us through the offer of the gospel. When Christ and all of his benefits are extended in the gospel, it is as if Christ's heart is also put forward. The divine forgiveness of sins is not a cold, mechanical religious transaction but the pulsating heart of Christ offering life and love to otherwise helpless and hopeless people. This is why rejecting the gospel is so serious. To do so is not just to reject religion but to reject a person. Rejecting the gospel is refusing Christ and his love.

Not only is rejecting Christ an insult to his love, but it's also a proclamation of one's own sufficiency. Such a person considers the gospel unnecessary. This is similar to Naaman, the Syrian commander, who thought washing in the Jordan River seven times to be cleansed was beneath him (2 Kings 5:1–14). It's humiliating to own the truth that you are a sinner who's unable to offer God anything of value and to wholly depend on his gracious love.

The writer of Hebrews explains the dire consequences of rejecting Christ: "How shall we escape if we neglect such a great salvation?" (Heb. 2:3). To *neglect* is to disregard or not pay attention to something. We do this every day when the mail is delivered. We sift through the envelopes and disregard the unimportant pieces. To "neglect such a great salvation" means that one deems Christ and his gospel as unimportant and unnecessary. It's like marking the message of the gospel as spam. Why would someone do this? Because, like junk mail or spam email, the gospel message is not compelling to him. Christ's heart for sinners doesn't move the needle for this person. There are more important matters to consider.

In Hebrews 10, the author further describes what it looks like to reject the gospel: such a person has "trampled underfoot the Son of God, and has profaned the blood of the covenant" (Heb. 10:29). This is a gripping visual. Think of what happens when you trample seed into the ground (Luke 8:5) or when pigs trample anything in a pigsty (Matt. 7:6). In both cases, there's little regard for the value of whatever is underfoot. But there's another nuance to the word translated as "trampled." It can mean "to look on with scorn" or "treat with disdain."[3] To reject the gospel of Christ is to treat the Christ of the gospel with scornful contempt. To do so disregards him and diminishes all that he has done, considering his death of no value.

What can one expect who has so rejected and repudiated Christ's self-giving love? Judgment. There's "a fearful expectation of judgment, and a fury of fire that will consume the adversaries" (Heb. 10:27). Or as the author says earlier, "How shall we escape if we neglect such a great salvation?" (2:3). People may escape from the great prisons of the world, but there is no escape from the dungeon of damnation, where the warden is the judge (see Rev. 14:10). He is also the Savior whose love was rejected. "He that dies for slighting love, sinks deepest into hell, and will there be tormented by the remembrance of that evil, more than by the deepest cogitation of all his other sins. Take heed, therefore; do not make love thy tormentor, sinner."[4]

Consider Him Again

Consider again Christ's sobering words on the last day: "For whoever is ashamed of me and of my words, of him will the Son

---

3 "Καταπατέω" in Walter Bauer, *A Greek-English Lexicon of the New Testament and Other Early Christian Literature*, ed. Frederick W. Danker, 3rd ed. (Chicago: University of Chicago Press, 2000), 523.

4 John Bunyan, *The Jerusalem Sinner Saved*, in *The Works of John Bunyan*, ed. George Offor, 3 vols. (Edinburgh: Banner of Truth Trust, 1991), 1:69.

of Man be ashamed when he comes in his glory and the glory of the Father and of the holy angels" (Luke 9:26). If you reject him now, he'll reject you then. But it's not too late. If you are reading these words, then the door of mercy is still flung open wide. Trust and treasure this glorious Savior!

Consider again his worth; instead of devaluing his glory, make much of it. Think on his authority; instead of rejecting his lordship, submit to it. Notice again his heart; instead of neglecting his salvation, receive it. He's not ashamed of people like you and me. He's willing to have you.

That is, if he's not beneath you.

General Index

Scripture Index

Also Available from Erik Raymond

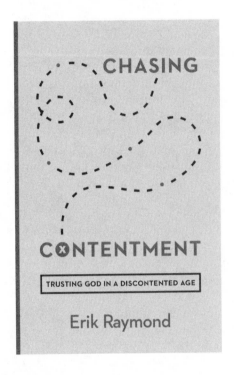

In this practical and encouraging book, Erik Raymond establishes what contentment is and how to learn it, teaching us to trust in the God who keeps his promises rather than our changing circumstances.

For more information, visit **crossway.org**.